ERIN BLOOM DAVENPORT

SHORT SWEET & SACRED

52 UPLIFTING STORIES
FROM LIFE COACHES WHO OVERCAME AND MOVED FROM STUCK TO SUCCESS

Published by Elevate Publishing, Roswell, Georgia

ISBN 978-0-9976215-5-6 (print)

Printed in the United States of America

This book is dedicated to the part of all of us that is seeking an even more fulfilling, purposeful, and joy filled life. A warm thank you to every life coach who openly shares their stories within these pages. Sharing a glimpse of your journey is what brings this book to life.

Contents

Introduction

Many of us find ourselves busy with the daily hustle, but at the same time, longing for our inner cup to be filled with inspiration. Within these pages are 52 short and sweet stories intended to bring you a quick dose of inspiration while showcasing the sacred journeys of 52 authentic life coaches from all over the world.

This book was dreamt up and written so it could find you. The beautiful soul who wants to deeply believe there is more to life. The overcomer desiring hope who is sick and tired of feeling sick and tired. The heart-centered go-getter who has a few more hurdles to jump on the way to success.

This book is intended to hug your heart with a warm welcome. Everyone who was selected to contribute understands the meaning behind the word "struggle." And we aren't afraid to be honest and share about our real-life experiences so that you can borrow our hope and see the possibilities for breakthrough. We are all here to tell you it is possible to live a life that brings you joy—just as we have discovered.

The stories you will soon encounter include topics surrounding marriage, death, divorce, illness, self-discovery, career changes, victories for minorities, mental health, divine timings, and the list goes on.

There is an eye-opening message for everyone within this book. During a few stories, you might not relate, but you can still appreciate the writer's journey. And what I use as a guideline for my life is this—take what resonates and leave the rest. This is an empowering way to listen to someone's unique viewpoint while having receptivity to see what is personally beneficial. I welcome you to do the same if needed.

What makes this book one-of-a-kind is that you will get to hear from a diverse group of wonderful people with varying beliefs and viewpoints in spirituality. We show the beauty in uniting and sharing our stories as a powerful force for good.

To gently invite you to put yourself in the shoes of the writer, terms like Higher Power, a Still Small Voice, the Infinite, and the Universe are found throughout the following stories. This book is not to showcase what exactly we believe, but rather, the value of believing within itself. Inclusivity was at the forefront of our minds as this book was being put together.

As an international speaker, transformational life coach, and previous therapeutic wilderness guide, I have walked with an assortment of people during their journeys to greatness by offering techniques, tools, and understanding.

Not only am I qualified on paper, but I have also experienced grief, been a defeater of the statistics that could have held my future hostage, and been a divorcee, a past overachiever painfully underachieving, a survivor of abuse, and the list goes on. And you better believe I have a burning desire in my soul and an ever-fueled longing to make sure that every human being on this planet knows they are not alone in their past or current struggles.

As you make your way through this book, I request one thing—have an open mind. Oftentimes, as we spend more time on this planet and come across hardships, it can become easier and easier to tell ourselves why we can't, why it won't work, or assume we are not the special one that ends up happy at the end. If you relate to any of this, it's time for a mindset makeover.

I am going to whole-heartedly invite you to take all the doubts and concerns you may have and put them to the side. Where your attention goes, your energy flows. So why not divert your precious energy to what you would love to experience instead? There is no need to figure out the "how it's going to work" for this stretch of your journey. Be open to the possibilities for your own personal transformation.

What may seem like a coincidental unearthing of this book, I assure you it has more depth than you can imagine. Moments of coming across things that are "out of the blue" are in reality the calling of your heart colliding with what it has been searching for. In this case, the call is being answered by the inspiration and positivity you will find within *Short, Sweet & Sacred*.

Enjoy your journey as you immerse yourself within these pages. You will soon see how taking a few minutes of regular reading can change the way you see the world around you, your circumstances, and your future. I am holding the best for you!

—Erin Davenport

Choosing a Different Path

Erin Davenport

UTAH, USA

"You better take a photo of us because I am not wearing this ever again," I say with a slightly bratty tone that is tinted with endearment. My dad and I have Iowa-style button-up coveralls on to protect us from the winter cold. And my sister is snapping a quick picture of us to commemorate the rare occasion. I am not the farm coverall "type," but my dad is adamant about showing me his deer tracking camera he has set up on the other side of the property.

Being a vegetarian, I am not excited about the idea of tracking deer, but I am trying to be supportive of my dad's new hobby. It's been a few years since he has had any joy in his life. He's never been the same since he hurt his knee at work. He's only 52 years old. It's hard to watch this marathon runner of the past walking with a hobble, a cane, and struggling with his health. Hopefully, me tagging along can add some excitement to his Christmas day. He has the biggest smile, and I am hoping to catch a glimpse of it during our father-daughter bonding time.

Walking into the mudroom, I pull on a pair of my dad's over-sized rubber boots, and I poke each of my fingers into my gloves. I announce, "I think I have everything!" My dad walks from the kitchen to join me and opens the creaky screen door.

Outside, the sun is warm and inviting, the ground is covered with at least five inches of snow, and we ready for our mini adventure. My dad leads the way from the porch onto the snow-blanketed ground. As he walks, he leaves behind his size 13 footprints in the snow. I am thinking, *Thank you, Dad. You just made my life easier.* I start putting my oversized boots into the footprints he leaves behind. Since I am wearing a pair of his boots, they fit perfectly with each step. *Crunch. Crunch. Crunch.* I make my way through the snow after my dad.

My mind drifts as I think about how magical it is to literally be following in my dad's footsteps. As I am having this whimsical thought, I hear a clear and calm voice enter my mind. "You don't want to follow in your father's footsteps." I stop dead in my tracks. As I hesitate, I wonder where that voice came from. It's the strangest thought because here I am enjoying my dad's company, he's smiling for the first time in months, and I have a thought that goes against everything I am experiencing in this moment. Yet I can't shake it free.

Pushing away the unexpected message, I catch up to my dad, and we start chatting about my year at college. My dad shares, "I am proud of you. It sounds like school is going good for you, and it's neat how you are taking so many opportunities to travel." My heart swells. My dad's loving words mean the world to me.

Slightly out of breath, we arrive at the property fence that is lined with trees, and I can see the deer camera strapped to a post. "Next to the post here, you see this gap in the fence? These are the deer tracks from when they travel this route. And hopefully this camera is going to show me how often they are coming through and how many there are," my dad says as he unstraps the camera and puts it under his arm to carry home.

"By the way, the only type of deer shooting I will be doing is with my Nikon," I say playfully. My dad laughs, and we continue back home enjoying our special time together.

Six days later on New Year's Eve, I am at the convention center in Baltimore representing my college as a recruiter. Three of us young ladies are excitedly engaging with each passerby. I am enjoying every minute of it!

The recruiting director edges her way through the crowd to our booth. "Hey everyone! Let's take a break for today. There is a historical shipyard nearby that will be splendid for great photos," she says as she turns towards me. I light up! Everyone knows how much I love photography. We gather our purses as our director puts a "Be back!" sign on the table.

At the shipyard, there is so much to see amongst the beautifully manicured landscape and treasures of the past. My friends pose for photos next to the canons, and we have a great time being silly. After what feels like a few hours, we start walking back to the car while I am enjoying my photo previews on my camera. There are so many great shots.

Everyone piles into the car, and then silence. The recruiting director turns herself towards me from the driver's seat and puts her hand on my knee. I start to see sadness wash away the joy on everyone's faces. "Your dad passed away this morning," the director shares.

I feel a flood of panic. "My dad or my step-dad? Which one passed away?" I frantically ask. I feel like I can't breathe.

"Your dad. Your brother found him this morning. He tried to revive him. They think he died from heart complications. I am so, so, so sorry. We brought you here because we wanted to give you good memories from the trip before we broke the news. We are here for you." I burst out sobbing. A river of tears flows down my face.

Resting my head on my friend's shoulder in the backseat, I continue to cry with an aching that goes so deep within me that it feels like it never ends. My mind is racing. And then I remember that unexpected voice from six days ago saying, "You don't want to follow in your father's footsteps." I cry even harder.

It has felt like my life has been marred by struggles, obstacles, and getting stuck over and over again. And when I look at my dad's life, I see the same story. It is heart-wrenching to think about how talented my dad was and how he would never have a chance to live the life of his dreams. His time is over. I know he died as a person suffering while getting by day to day and not knowing how to do any better. Maybe this is my wake-up call. I start to think about my unhealthy habits, my compulsions, my anxiety, and my relationship choices. Talk about a mess. I have been settling in so many ways by living in default, much like my dad, despite our best intentions.

During the car ride, I decide that I am going to cherish those final moments I had with my dad on that special day. And I am also going to take to heart the message that was gifted to me. A message that inspires me to carve my own path with intention. My dad's life may not have been as fulfilled as he had hoped. But I can use this experience to fuel my passion for creating a life I love. The type of life where I look forward to jumping out of bed. The type of life I can be proud of. For me. And in honor of my dad.

An Angel and Best Friend

Laura Walker
TEXAS, USA

The cool morning air blows across my face. Excitement and urgency surge through my body as I click the remote to the garage door and watch for the door to close. Backing out of the driveway of our suburban home, I head out to complete a myriad of tasks and chores that make up a mom's daily to-do list! It is the first day of school in suburban Fort Worth, Texas. I am so happy to have successfully fed, clothed, supplied-up, and ushered my tribe of four kiddos off to their respective schools without a hitch. Yes, I know. I am bragging a bit. *Wink. Wink.*

Now it's time to run a few errands to restock the fridge, work from my home office, and be ready to hear their first day of school shenanigans in a few short hours when they arrive back home! I plan to be prepared with fresh baked cookies in hand, ready and waiting.

As I turn down an adjacent street, I notice a woman standing at the end of her driveway. She is standing precariously at the junction of her driveway and the street, staring off down the sidewalk that runs the length of the street towards the elementary school. She is sobbing. I see tears streaming down her face and her body shuddering with sobs.

Wait! I recognize her! It is coming back to me! We briefly met months before at a neighborhood garage sale. Immediately, I pull over to check on her. The excitement I was feeling mere moments ago is now gone as I am saddened by what I see.

Pulling my SUV up, I roll down the window and ask, "Hi, oh my gosh. What's wrong, Amy? That is your name, right? What is wrong?" She is crying uncontrollably. Part of me is sincerely concerned and part of me scared about her reply after observing her current emotional status. Words tumble out of her mouth like a verbal waterfall.

"Yes, it's Amy," she says between the cascade of tears, with what I can hardly call a smile. "I am late to work. My boss is going to kill me. My husband starts a new job today, and he couldn't take my daughter to her first day of preschool. So, I took her to school and made it back, but now I missed my son leaving for his first day of first grade. And he went on his bike alone!" she manages to barely get out, choking on sobs between the words. "I just do not know what I'm going to do every day to get my kids to school!" she says as she cries inconsolably.

My heart stops. As a mom, I get it! Empathy washes over me, and I identify with this woman's situation in this very moment more than she can imagine. Memories flood my mind and heart of earlier years of my own life. Mental images jolt through my mind and burn my heart. I had been a single mom in a small town. I had three children under the age of ten years attending three different schools with two different start times and no one to help. Those days were hard. So hard!

In that split second, a still small voice said, "Be her angel. She needs you." Turning off my SUV, I open the door and throw my arms around Amy. Hugging her, I say, "Don't you worry about one thing! I got this, sister! Send your sweet kids to my house every morning, and I will make sure that they are fed and taken to school on time each day. Sometimes it takes a village, and I am here to help you!"

Amy's sobs stop abruptly, the tears end, and a tiny smile of gratitude begins to curve up on the outer edges of her mouth. "Are you sure? I couldn't impose like that. Oh my gosh. Thank you. Thank you. Thank you! You are a lifesaver!" Amy shouts.

"Amy, life isn't happening to us. It is happening through us," I reply. "If I didn't take this opportunity to help you right now, then I wouldn't be living a life that I believe in! It is the least I can do, one mom to another. I have been exactly where you are, and you need help. Let me help you!" With a big hug and deep sigh, Amy dries her eyes and agrees to my offer.

Driving away, I see Amy get into her car, take a deep breath, and back out of her driveway, and she is finally on her way to work. She is late, but never late again if I can help it. I know deep in my soul that this is the beginning of a beautiful friendship that will stand the test of time for years to come!

Immediately an overwhelming sense of gratitude wells up inside of me! Tears of joy sting my eyes as gratitude engulfs my heart. Gratitude to be in the right place at the right time. A gratitude to be in tune enough to hear the calling of the greater good. And gratitude to serve in a heart-centered way—to a mother who was in need on the first day of school.

It is now so many years later. Our kids have graduated high school, and Amy and I have shared many tears, laughs, birthdays, holidays, and more than a few glasses of wine! Stopping that day to help a distraught woman in the street was absolutely one of the best decisions of my life. That soft voice that implored me to help Amy was guiding me to my forever best friend. For that, I will forever be grateful.

My Crossroad Moment

Rajika Mahan
VIRGINIA, USA

For me, I have everything I can ever want. This includes a beautiful house, three beautiful kids, being married to a wonderful man for 25 years, and having the opportunity to stay home to care for my family. But on the inside, I feel anything but happy. I am at the lowest point of my life.

I have feelings of frustration and dissatisfaction with myself, but I continue to ignore it because it's so deeply painful. My time and energy are completely centered around my kids, my husband, and my in-laws. I know I am trying to fill the void of feeling inadequate and unworthy. Each day, I barely get by, and at the end of the day, I find myself lying in bed crying and thinking about how to find an answer to what will bring me joy, fulfillment, and purpose.

The sleepless nights are impacting my daily life, leading me to have conversations while being irritated and in a bad mood. My kids and my husband ask me time and time again if they have done something wrong. They ask, "Did we upset you in any way?" I snap at them and say, "NO!"

Deep within, there is a feeling that I cannot express outwardly. But today, it is apparent to me that I am totally checked out from my relationships. Every conversation I have with my husband, kids, and in-laws ends up in arguments or one of us walking away because we are frustrated with each other. I am at my wit's end!

Today I decide, even though I am scared to bring it up, to have a conversation with my husband. I am unhappy, and I know he feels the same way. We tell our parents we are going out for a drive, and we will be back shortly. My request to talk is going to lead to a turning point for me since I am going to openly share what is on my heart. I want more joy and peace of mind, and this is my chance to see what I can do about it.

As we are traveling away from home, I muster up the courage to have the conversation. As I begin, it's uncomfortable and very emotional for me. My spoken thoughts feel like I am vomiting out my many feelings.

My husband listens to me patiently, and now it's his turn. My heart sinks because I am scared of what he is going to say. He expresses how he is unhappy and frustrated, and he shares, "Everything I do doesn't seem to be enough." He is discouraged every day when he walks into the house because he doesn't know what mood I am going to be in.

He says, "Sometimes I think about not coming home. And despite everything I am doing, I can't make you happy, and it's just not enough. The kids are not happy, and I notice how the atmosphere in the house changes, especially when you are in a mood. I love you, but I don't think we make each other happy. Perhaps the best thing is for us to separate and evaluate the situation." I am not surprised by what he is sharing as I know it is a long time coming.

This is my first time sharing my genuine feelings of frustration, anger, and unhappiness. I have enjoyed raising our kids, and I have had the privilege of being home with them. But beneath it all, our relationship is on autopilot, and we are living our lives as roommates.

We both want it to work, and one option we explore is marriage counseling. It is uncomfortable for both of us because, culturally, counseling is frowned upon, and it's something couples don't do. As each session starts, we share what has happened, and then our therapist shares her insights and suggestions on how to approach the situation. There are a few bumpy days because it is all new to us, and it's awkward to tell someone else our problems. But we try.

My expectation of therapy is to help me fix my husband and me. I want therapy to help me resolve my internal feelings, but as I continue down this path, it leaves me even more resentful.

Fast forward. One day, my husband comes home and shares with me that he isn't willing to go back because it's not helping. He tells me, "It's not going to work, and if you want to go, you can go by yourself." I am furious. I desperately want him to see my point of view, and I want him to understand that this is the only option to save our marriage.

I continue to go, committing that I am not going to give up. If nothing else, I am attending sessions so I can get insight into what is missing for us. I give it another six months, and I am still not seeing an improvement. During all of this, I do have my faith in my higher power. I have complete faith that there is another way, and I know my creator will help me in my search.

One evening, my friend calls me and invites me to a presentation, and I share I would love to attend with her. As we walk into the event, it is a full house with over 150 people. I sit in the back row with my hands folded, not knowing what to expect. The speaker starts to share how we have an opportunity to create new possibilities, and he elaborates on what stops most people from taking the first step.

He is talking about how humans attach meaning to events, and then they carry that interpretation into every interaction. He shares, "We can learn to let go of these attached meanings and recognize that, in fact, it's not true. It's at that point we can change our lives, and life can be full of new adventures and possibilities." This intrigues me, and I want to know more.

At the end, they make an offer to sign up for the course, and I jump out of my seat to register. I put it on my calendar while committing to be there for the full weekend so I can understand why I am so unhappy.

As the weekend event finishes, I start to implement what I learned. I find myself in a happier place. I am able to express myself more, and I have more courage to share my feelings. My internal shift helps with the atmosphere in the home, and it is getting easier to have more joyful conversations.

I am happy to share that my husband and I have recently celebrated 29 years of marriage. I sit back and reflect on my journey, how this was a wake-up call for me and how I had put my most important relationships on the back burner. Today, I can fully recognize that there is a reason I went through this. It was there for me to grow and expand my awareness so that I could create a life I love today—a life full of peace and happiness.

Autumn

Golivia Lee
MASSACHUSETTS, USA

It's a typical day in autumn when I am looking through the window of the car. The fine raindrops and the autumn breeze unite on the cold glass window right before my eyes. While I trace their path with my fingertips, I suddenly hear a mumbling voice. "Look at those trees. They look so awful. All of the leaves are gone, and all there is left are empty branches. I prefer spring or summer. Even winter has its charm, but autumn just looks depressing."

A deep sigh follows their freed expression. "I actually think it looks beautiful," I reply. "Tell me, what makes it so beautiful to you?" Blue asks, intrigued. A little spark of curiosity fills the air while I take a deep breath of appreciation.

"These trees were once filled with beautiful leaves, and some may even have borne fruit. The trees give unconditionally, and by the time autumn arrives, they have given all they can give. No matter the weather, they keep standing tall. Some will break, and some will fall. They stay grounded while adjusting and adapting themselves to every season.

They are gentle warriors who have given their all, wearing their scars and wrinkles proudly. Some are hidden. They'd rather break than bow. Autumn gives them permission to shed what no longer serves them. A time when it is okay to let go and reenergize. So, when it is time to bloom again, the trees stay grounded in knowing that having leaves or fruit does not determine their worth as they are perfect in every way. Complete in every form. Grounded and forever connected with Mother Nature."

Peaceful silence fills the car. The view around us has colored itself with shades of gratitude. A moment of relief occurs within me. An opportunity to choose what serves me remains. We arrive at our destination at the end of our drive. While Blue stays in the car, I close the door behind me. Finally, everything makes sense. Wings of color take flight and fill the realm of my mind again, flapping in unison and whispering, "I Am Enough."

The Visit

Darla Evon
KANSAS, USA

I am sitting in my car crying, not knowing what to expect. What would it be like? Will I be in danger? What will he be like now? The thoughts run wildly through my mind as I dry my tears. It is time to go in.

Walking up the sidewalk to the prison on this cold winter day, it feels like the longest and coldest walk of my entire life. The barbed wire fencing, the electric gates, the video cameras, emotionless guards in their uniforms—this all feels surreal. Never in my lifetime did I think I would be going inside prison walls. Never did I imagine visiting my firstborn son here.

Once inside, I take off my shoes and send them through the metal detector. Next, I get the full pat down—the guard feels under my bra, my pockets are turned inside out, I stick out my tongue as they look inside my mouth, guards check the soles of my feet, and finally, I stand with my legs in a V-shape and arms out like a cross as they check for contraband. As a last precaution, I am thoroughly sniffed by a trained dog.

Feeling like the prisoner, I head into a holding room between cement walls and two more locked doors. I am freezing, and it smells like an old musty basement inside. I hear a loud buzz, and the giant metal door slides open. The guard inside directs me to sit at a table with two chairs.

Tears keep falling, and I can't stop them. I notice a few games sitting on a nearby table that can be checked out, and there are several vending machines with processed food and soda. On the bare cement wall next to my table hangs a clock. I swear time is standing still while I am waiting. About thirty visitors are also sitting in their assigned chairs, waiting like I am.

After what felt like hours, I see my son walking in with five other prisoners. He is wearing green pants and a matching shirt with tan work boots. Our eyes lock as he walks over. We give one another a hug for probably two seconds before a guard says that is long enough. We sit knee-to-knee across from each other at the table. I can't take my eyes off of him.

He interrupts the silence and says, "Mom, don't cry. I'm okay." I reaffirm to myself that he looks healthy, from my motherly perspective. We spend three hours talking and reminiscing together. He tells me stories, and I share a few with him. Oh, how I have missed him.

Looking around, I see other inmates playing checkers with their visitors. Oddly, it feels like a luxury to ask my son if I can buy his lunch from the vending machine. I have pretzels and water; he has a processed chicken sandwich and soda. This is our first meal together in over a year.

As a mom, all I want to do is love on him. I want to brush

the hair from his face and hug him and tell him how loved he is. It is different in here though. No touching and a two-foot table distance keeping us apart. Our conversation is touching for me though, deeper than any physical hug. We talk more about life, forgiveness, and moving on. We discuss how the next chapter in his life's book will read. Even though he is still locked up, it is time for him to move on in his mind and to make plans about what the rest of his life and what that can look like.

He has written me a lot of letters, and we have talked on the phone over the past year. But nothing can take the place of seeing my son. I feel so much gratitude to have this time, and I am simply grateful he is alive. He is the survivor of a drug addiction that almost cost him his life. It has taken prison to get him sober and to wake up. This is definitely one of his toughest lessons in his 27 years of life.

During his time in prison, he has grown up fast. He has to. And I know his creator is working on his heart to restructure his life. He has time to reflect, grow up, get sober, and learn a lot of lessons from witnessing things, which still to this day he doesn't talk about.

As a mother in this Colorado prison, my eyes are opened too. While I look around, all I see is love. A son visiting his dad, a wife visiting her lover, a grandparent visiting their grandson—love everywhere. There is no judgment here, just people loving each other right where they are. This moment in my life feels profound as I realize we are all one mistake away from being locked up too.

How many of us have done something that could have changed the trajectory of our lives? Today, I am soaking in this meaningful lesson about deep love and transformational forgiveness and non-judgment. We all matter. We are more alike than we are different.

We are worthy of love and second chances. People make mistakes. Knowing there are horrific offenders in prison, I am not being naïve. They, too, are someone's son or daughter, and I am choosing to hold on to that.

My sweet son starts to tell me about a few young men who have no family to answer their calls or write them. They are discarded as an embarrassment and given up on. After my son shares about these inmates and says they are a "safe connection," I immediately decide that I am going to write them letters, send them j-pay emails, and set up phone accounts so they can reach out to me. It means so much to me that these young men know at least one person in the outside world acknowledges their existence and that they matter.

Saying goodbye after our three-hour visit is not easy. Tears show up again, but my heart is grateful that I have had this time with my son today. Until the next time I can visit him, letters will have to fill that void. Our relationship is better than it has ever been. First, because the drugs are gone. And second, because we are mending and communicating in a way that most mothers and sons aren't typically interacting.

The power of the written word in letter form is powerful, and we are expressing sentiments that may have never been stated if he hadn't gone to prison. I would not wish this circumstance on anyone, and yet, I wouldn't change a thing. It has taken him a few years of sitting behind those prison walls to get clear on what matters in life. And as a mother, it is healing to know this is his journey in life, and the best I can do is love him from a distance while he does his time.

Rude Awakening

Samantha Kaaua
HAWAII, USA

The sound of my alarm goes off, and I jump out of bed with butterflies in my stomach and my thoughts racing a million miles a minute! It is 6 a.m. on a beautiful spring morning. After brushing my teeth and getting dressed, I walk downstairs to gather my things for this life-changing day. I have been preparing for this very day for the past two and a half years!

My heart is pounding, my mind is spinning, and a nervous excitement fills my body, knowing that I am so close to the finish line! The past two years have been treacherous and challenging, to say the least. I gave birth to my third daughter, I had a heart procedure to fix my heart condition, and to top it all off, I was in my master's program to become a marriage and family therapist!

Today, it will all be over as I sit for eight hours taking my comprehensive exam to determine if I can graduate this summer. All of those late nights and long papers are over. I let out a sigh of relief as I reflect on the silly stories of grad school life, crazy study sessions, and even crazier client stories.

"Focus, Sam!" I say to myself out loud. "Make sure you bring everything you need for your exam today!" I go down the laundry list of items in my head: snacks—check, water—check, blanket—check. "Oh! A cooler," I say to myself as I begin searching through the cabinets for a small one to carry into the exam room.

"I found one, perfect!" As I open the cooler, I realize there is something inside. Hmmm, what's in this black box? As I open it, I am perplexed. I walk over to the living room where my husband is sitting on the couch and ask him with a disgusted look on my face, "What is this?"

Everything starts to move in slow motion, and the confusion hits me like a ton of bricks. My husband looks at me in utter shock, and his face goes pale as if he has seen a ghost. I ask him again with even more confusion, "What is it?" My husband begins to sob uncontrollably, and life itself seems to come to a screeching halt. I know what it is. "Oh my God! Is this what I think it is?" I say with anger and disgust this time.

Silence. There is only silence. He doesn't need to say anything. I know what it is. It's his weed! You see, this isn't just your recreational weed or your medicinal marijuana weed. This is a symbol of something so much bigger than that!

This is ten years of my husband lying to my face, day in and day out, about his addiction. This is him choosing to sleep downstairs because the couch was "more comfortable" than our bed. This is him passing out at 4 o'clock every afternoon and acting grouchy and short-tempered with me and the girls. This is ten years of lies!

My eyes close as my heart sinks into my stomach. "What's

happening right now? What's going on? This is not happening today!" I say to myself in frustration and rage.

I open my eyes. I look straight into my husband's tear-filled eyes, and I see the terror that is running through his entire body. I know my husband is stuck. Not only mentally and emotionally, but he is physically stuck! It was only six days ago that he was rushed to the emergency room for a work accident that almost took his entire foot off.

As I glare into his soul, my body begins to tremble, heat rises up from inside of me, and I say to him with pure rage, "You are so lucky that you're hurt right now! How dare you? How can you? How can you do this to me? What are you thinking?!"

And then a tsunami of emotions hit me. My eyes well up, and I burst into tears. My mind is going back and forth in all directions. "How could I be so stupid? There is no way I am going to pass my exam now. I don't even deserve to be a marriage and family therapist! Look at my relationship. It's a mess! I'm a mess! How am I going to help anyone?! This is my fault too!"

In total defeat, I sink into the couch next to my husband. The pain in my chest is no longer from my heart condition. This pain is worse. The pain in my chest is the effect of being absolutely heartbroken. I feel betrayed, hurt, and angry all at the same time.

As we sit in silence for what feels like hours, but really was only a few minutes, a calmness comes over me. A new part of me emerges that I didn't even know exists. I have an exam to pass. All of a sudden, I hear a new kind of voice in my head. *"You are wiser, you are focused, and you are ready to begin a new chapter in your life."* This calm, confident voice says in encouragement, *"YOU DESERVE TO BE HAPPY!"* At this very moment, I vow that I am not a victim of my relationships anymore! I have three beautiful girls to raise. And no matter what happens today, I DO deserve to be happy!

As I stand up from the couch and walk out the door, I leave the old part of me behind.

Be Confident! Be Courageous!

Ivery De La Cruz
TEXAS, USA

It's my first day of school this year. Everyone is up early, and the excitement is flowing through the house. I am getting dressed, getting lunch, and we four girls are having our hair combed. I am too excited to eat. Not only is it the first day of school, but it is the first day of elementary school integration for Dallas Independent School District in Texas. Seagoville ISD was annexed into Dallas ISD this year. Integration means that black and white students are going to the same school for the first time in this area.

I am so excited thinking about a playground with swings, sliding boards, a merry-go-round, and see-saws. At my old elementary school, there were no such things. We had trees, a creek, and rocks. We could look across the fence into the white schoolyard and see the children playing on their decorative and fun equipment. I'm sure they could see us running around the trees and jumping over the creek. As a rising fifth grader, these are my thoughts about going to the "white" school.

The school bus is coming, and everyone is making a mad dash to get out of the house. My dad stops me, takes me by the hand, and looks me in the eyes as he says, "Ivery Nell, those white children might be further along in their books than you, but remember, you are just as smart as they are. Don't hold your tongue. You are just as good as they are." During this moment I feel something inside. Almost as if I swallowed his words. I don't quite understand them, but somehow, I know they are important. I dash to the bus and I head to my new school.

Throughout school, I have always been a great student, friendly, and teachers have taken an interest in me for leadership roles. I am involved in many activities, including band, chess club, the science club, student council, medical careers club, Spanish club, drama club, and on top of all of that, I work in a home for handicapped children. You might label me as an overachiever.

One evening, I am telling my dad about my school activities and he takes my hand and looks into my eyes and says, "Ivery Nell, they took the reins off the horse (referring to the integration) but they left the bit in its mouth." I feel angry because it seems like he is taking back his words that I am good enough. It takes me a long time to realize what he means. It's his way of telling me that I will never be completely free to do what I want. That being black is the bit in my mouth, and that someone will always control how far I can go.

I choose to believe I can open these closed doors and break through these glass ceilings. My father gives me a great gift that day as I am rushing out the door and thinking of playing on the swings in the schoolyard. He instills in me a sense of confidence and courage to see beyond appearances and circumstances. That confidence and courage, along with hard work, taking risks, and listening to those who encourage me, empowers me to never stop believing that I can achieve anything.

This seed planted, so long ago, has been watered and nurtured by so many along my journey. This growth is allowing me to touch thousands of lives as a college graduate and registered nurse in hospitals and other institutions.

As a United States Army Chaplain for 25-years, I travel around the world ministering to the military, their family members, government employees, and civilian nationals in each country I visit. I also teach, supervise, and certify chaplains and pastors in clinical pastoral education specialization. This certification allows them to work as chaplains in hospital and institutions.

Yes, there are moments when others want to control me and stop my progress. One early issue is while seeking ordination. It is a credential I need to be hired as a hospital chaplain. The Convention does not ordain women to the ministry. But the churches within the Convention are autonomous bodies and can choose to do so. As word gets around the seminary that I am seeking ordination, I overhear one male student ask another one, "What do you think about Ivery Dotson wanting to get ordained?" The other student replies, "I don't know. If it is of God, it will stand."

I make an appointment and talk to my pastor about getting ordained. He is excited and agrees immediately to do it next Wednesday night. The church staff are not so excited, and the deacons state, "No. What if she wants to become a pastor? We will be the laughingstock of the Convention." That Wednesday night, one person is ordained for ministry, and it is not me. I congratulate the new minister and cry in the car all the way home from church. My heart aches at this perceiving loss of my ministry.

Listening to the still small voice within me, I join another church that hired me as youth pastor and says yes, "We will ordain you to the ministry." I am elated! I am paid $10.00 a week as a youth pastor. This position and salary meet the requirements of a "salaried ministry position," which allows me to go on active duty in the Army as a chaplain.

After retiring from the Army, that seed of confidence and courage my father planted in me so long ago, is still growing and flourishing today. Teaching underserved high school students in health careers fuels my passion and allows me to pass the baton of courage and confidence.

Many of these students are going on to college and beyond, touching lives in medicine, pharmacy, physical therapy, nursing, and many other fields. One student asks me to be her recommender for the Gates Millennium Scholarship. I write her recommendation and she is awarded a full ride scholarship from bachelor to doctoral degree!

I believe my life's mission was given to me during my first day of fifth grade. Be confident! Be courageous. I share this enthusiasm and strive to plant this seed in all areas of my life, which includes being a transformational life coach. Helping people see beyond limiting beliefs, appearances, and circumstances—to live a life they love!

Unexpected Connection

Arehn McCarty

OREGON, USA

What a day! I am flying high because I am presenting on stage at a national conference. I share my dreams and plans for my career with leaders from all over the country. The chance to reach so many influential people in one go is a springboard for my entire future. With everyone here, I know I am making the perfect networking connection. I am excited, alive, and pumped from the day.

At the end of the event, it's late at night, and everyone has gone their separate ways. As I practically skip to my car, I notice the parking lot is empty and a misty rain is coming down. The day's official program was over hours ago.

I open the driver's side door, get in, start the car, check the mirrors, and put the car in reverse, all the while thinking about how special the day has been. I feel so competent and professional in my best outfit and bright blue wool coat. I am sure this conference will give me the opportunity to make a connection and get my dream job!

As I start to drive away, I hear *thump, thump, thump*. I am not sure what it is, but I know it's not right. I get out and look at the car. I have a flat tire! It's dark and wet, and I am dressed to the nines. I feel as deflated as the tire. I don't even know if I have a jack, and I certainly don't have AAA.

I am the kind of person who likes to do everything herself. I am proud of my self-sufficiency and competence, and I really don't like asking for help. I don't want to ask anybody to do this for me. I don't even know if anyone is still here. I was just talking to Jim, the sound engineer, about the recordings of today's conference. With this hope in mind, I rush back to see if I can catch Jim before he leaves.

I have known Jim in passing for years. There are not too many people in their twenties working here, so we stand out. I have asked him a few times to join groups of us after work, but he has never come along with us. I don't know him except for an occasional "Good morning." I feel uncomfortable asking him for help. If he were a close friend, it might be easier. But I don't seem to have a choice if I want to get home tonight.

As I make my way, I see he is still here! He is standing a little hunched in the studio doorway. Feeling nervous, I peek in and sheepishly say, "I have a flat tire." Jim quickly says, "Do you want some help?"

As we walk to the car, my heart rate is speeding up as I keep babbling "Thanks" and saying obvious things like "It's late," "It's raining," and ridiculous things like "I didn't know the tire was going to do that." Jim is calm, easy-going, and straightforward about helping me.

He jacks up the car, takes the lug nuts off, pulls off the tire, puts the spare tire on, and lowers the car. And that's when we find that the spare is flat too. I feel a knot in my stomach as I think about how Jim is seeing my tires in such a state. I hate being seen as someone who doesn't take care of things.

He isn't flustered that he has a new problem to deal with this late at night. He has such an accepting presence. His relaxed body language tells me that this problem is easily solved and it's no big deal, even though he just wasted 20 minutes getting dirty in the rain putting on a flat spare.

He has a can of "fix a flat" at his house that we can put in the tire, and I can use that to get home. He drives us to his place, which is about ten minutes away. The dark surrounding us makes me feel like we are enclosed in a tiny windowless room. While we are in the strangely silent space of his car, the muffled sound of the road beneath us, the windshield wipers swishing, I fiddle with my purse strap and ask a lot of questions about him.

I am nervous and worried about his judgment of me. This time gives me the opportunity to get to know him a little bit. He plays Ultimate Frisbee (the only sport I've ever played) and has a great sense of humor and a wonderful laugh. I hadn't known anything about him before. We had only said "hi" as we passed in the halls these last three years. As I'm talking and listening, a thought crosses my mind. "I kind of like this guy."

We return to my car, and he puts the foam in the tire. He's doing all of this for me while I am standing around with my hands in my pockets, shifting from foot to foot, embarrassed and thankful. I say good night and drive home in the rain.

It's the next day, March 4th, which is the only day of the year that has a statement behind it—to march forth, to go forth. The conference ends early today, and I have decided to ask Jim out to dinner using the excuse of thanking him for fixing my tire. As I ask him, he says, "No, no, it's fine. I was happy to do it. You don't need to do that." I reply, "No, I really would like to take you out to thank you." After a few more denials, I think he finally gets it and says, "Oh, okay." After the day's conference, we go to a restaurant and talk.

Two hours later, we figure we should probably leave but don't want the night to end. We are enjoying each other's company so much that we go to a little park and talk some more. He's funny, thoughtful, kind, and we share so many interests. I never would have known who he was had I not had that flat tire, and I am so grateful.

As we are chatting in the park, it's getting late, and the policeman tells us the park is closed and we have to leave. We still don't want this to end. We've been married now for 27 years. And our time together is still amazing.

Donuts and Destiny

Christal Brown
VERMONT, USA

I am on my way to Dunkin Donuts. I've just taken another ride past my new house that's being built, and I am so grateful for the builder's hard work that I asked if they would like coffee. It's March in Vermont, the wind is whipping, and these guys are wearing at least three layers. Coffee is the least I can do.

Once I return and give them my offering of gratitude—two boxes of coffee and a dozen assorted donuts—I head back to work. I am compelled to honor their labor because the home that's being built isn't just shelter from the cold. It's the beginning of a new life. This house is going to be a fresh start for my son and me. We are currently living in the living room of an 800 square foot one-bedroom Bronx apartment. We are abiding in the living room while I rent out the bedroom to make ends meet. Moving to Vermont will be the beginning of a full-time position as a professor and the end of my part-time job status.

Being part-time meant renting rooms for months at a time

and commuting for 4.5 hours every other weekend. This transition marks the end of part-time daycare positions that I have to re-apply for each year. This will be the end of leading a dance company in New York City. This will be the end of a tumultuous relationship and the end of teaching dance to high schoolers.

There's just one problem. I don't yet have the money for the house that's being built. I gave the builder a deposit. Then I gave them my tax return in good faith, and I have a salary letter stating what I will be making when my full-time contract begins. But right now, I am a part-time visiting faculty member who makes the rest of her living as an artist. Banks don't like independent artists. I have been trying to get approved for a mortgage, but it hasn't come through yet. The builders have recommended banks, but no one has been able to make the numbers work.

I know this is my house. I designed it, I prayed for it, and I gave the builders donuts. When people ask me about the funding and other logistics about paying for the house, my response is, "I don't know. I'm waiting on God." Many respond with a quizzical look and then smile and nod. I know they think I'm crazy, but this is my truth. God tells me to get up from my desk in the fall and go find a house. I didn't find a house I liked, but I found a builder who said he would work with me. This is also not the first time I've purchased a home, so I am well versed in the rigor of financing.

It's been about four months, and I still haven't been approved for a loan. I don't have a down payment, and the only thing I know to do is pray. I get up from my prayer time, and the phone rings. It's the builder on the other end. He asks me if I know about these down payment grants from the local land trust. I say, "No, but if you point me in the right direction, I will fill it out right now."

I fill out the application, and a nice man named Terry McKnight calls me back. He explains what I suspected, that I don't qualify. But then he proceeds to ask me some very particular questions about my current situation that reframes my eligibility. He says he will be in touch.

Within a week, I go from having $400 to having a grant for a $40,000 down payment. I am approved for a mortgage! My son and I move to Vermont into the house that God built, and the angel who asked me those specific questions that got me qualified passes away soon after.

We all have a destiny, and it doesn't always make sense. And when I came to the end of my logic and I was searching for the next step, I offered the people involved some donuts, and I found the answers I was looking for.

This Scientist's Journey to "Do the Do"

Gina Eubank

TEXAS, USA

It's December 2003. In flannel jammies, I bend over the kitchen sink, incessantly vomiting. Both wrists restrained in braces, I grab for a glass of water. Unable to feel the glass in my hands, it shatters on the tile at my feet.

Blinded by tears, on my hands and knees, reaching into the oblivion of tears, blood, and shards, my back crashes into the kitchen cabinets as I sob, "How is this my life? How did I end up here? How is brain surgery even on the table as 'the next logical step for me'?" The small, still, resolute voice inside of me whispers, "We can do this, Gina!"

Through the soul-tormenting chaos, one thing is clear. Brain surgery will not be part of my life's story. With every part of my being, I know this is up to me and my Higher Power to end these ten years of suffering that I have endured.

As a pharmacist, the "scientifically proven" Western route has been my chosen path on this journey thus far. The supposed "winning combination," an 11-prescription drug recipe is failing me, and I am becoming sicker. Daily vomiting is absolutely exhausting. Doctors present brain surgery as the only remaining option they see for me.

This heart-wrenching moment, bloody on the kitchen floor, is when the paradigm flips. I make a firm decision to shift course and implement a totally new plan of action. The small, still voice I hear through terror and despair becomes my cardinal purpose: to heal, live, and thrive.

To truly live means listening. I am committed to building my relationship with my intuition and Higher Power. Not only do I follow this guidance, but I cherish it. I name the action steps I am prescribed by "The Whisper" as "Do the Do." My new level of awareness leads me to embrace my vocabulary of made-up phrases or Gina-isms.

Brain surgery is out of the question, so the Negative Nellie in my brain has to zip it and gets sent to the corner while I build my believing muscle and listen for "The Whisper." Now, I am uninhibited to conduct these Higher Power focus experiments.

My believing muscle grows robust in self-guided scientific research. I deduct that this connection and relationship with my Higher Power will consistently flourish if I stay calm and still, trust and have faith, and have the guts to follow through. In other words, to decide and take action.

The scientific method's first step is research. If guided, I read it. Self-discovery is part of this journey. I have listened to this voice before. It saved my hide when my parents wanted me home for curfew, supported me to pass exams, and led me as I trail-blazed professionally. What I didn't realize was its omnipresence. I decide, in the name of the scientific method, I will try everything I hear, as long as I can scientifically prove it won't hurt me. We are off on my healing journey!

Guided, I implement strategies by taking supplements, juicing, eating a vegan and alkaline diet, lymphasizing, using infrared sauna, colon hydrotherapy, and many more techniques. Even during mundane activities, I listen for "The Whisper" For instance, picking produce and parking. Standing in front of the avocados at the grocery store and hearing, "Look at the top and go three down, and there is your perfect avocado." And it works! As I look for a parking spot, I hear, "Turn here and look on the right," and lo and behold, there is a parking spot! As the procedure phase of my experiment continues, my body detoxes physically and emotionally.

My Higher Power wants me to make things sticky and easy to remember in terms of visualization. Life isn't always pretty as it comes together, but I know in my heart of hearts my healing is coming together. I decide to give myself grace. In every good story, there is a beginning, middle, and end.

If I had understood this before, I wouldn't have stayed in the middle so long. In the middle, I have been in a state of panic. A "10-Finger Spread" with both hands and all ten fingers spread, signifying stop. One day in the middle of a 10-Finger Spread, the "Gratitude High Five " is whispered to me as a solution.

Hands on my heart, I shut my eyes and slow down until all I feel is my heartbeat. Noticing only my heartbeat, I allow my brain to process how truly awesome life is. I can't tell my heart to stop beating, no matter how hard I try. I let this realization sink in. WOW! There is a power far greater than all I know in this world beating within my chest.

Breathing in through the nose and out through my mouth, I say, "Thank you." Five times I repeat this process, and then five times again. The way this sticks for me in my mind is that I envision myself giving my Higher Power a Gratitude High Five with both hands.

In my mind, it's the only logical counterbalance (antidote) to the 10-Finger Spread. The 10-Finger Spread stalls progress. The Gratitude High Five is a direct connection with my source, my Higher Power, in the most magnanimous form of praise—gratitude. The Gratitude High Five resets my calm button, and I hear the next step. I feel peace knowing more steps will be revealed after my next step.

Slowly, I taper off of the 11 prescriptions. There are difficult moments and difficult days. I'm on the bathroom floor with tear-drenched cheeks pressing on the cool tile, recovering from the most recent vomiting spell. I wonder if I am doing the right thing. And I know this is Negative Nellie. Ugh . . . I pull myself up with the aid of the toilet, and with determination, I wash my face, brush my hair, look in the mirror, and say, "Wow, I look terrible."

I grab my pen and paper. I begin writing my blessings, listing all of the steps taken and the progress I have made. Simply writing down these blessings reaffirms my faith and trust. I am on the right path! This is my "Truth is Game," and it puts Negative Nellie in her place! Boom! I am super excited and grateful to have a quick and efficient way to quiet Negative Nellie!

This starts the data collection phase with a daily ritual of Celebrating What Went Right Today! Any progress is progress! The key for me is to actually take note of any accomplishment, no matter how small.

Daily, I stack my wins and gain momentum on tapering the drugs. The pain is subsiding, and the vomiting is becoming less and less! Each day, my routine is focused on expecting "The Whisper," taking the action steps, stacking wins, my "Gratitude High Five," and putting Negative Nellie in her place with The Truth is Game.

Within eight months, I am HEALED. Astonished, doctors declare me a healing anomaly! No more headaches, no more vomiting, no more 11 prescription drugs, and no blurred vision from the tumor pressing on the optic nerve. I am tumor free and am so incredibly grateful I made the decision and the commitment to listen to "The Whisper!"

I Carry Your Heart
in My Head

Laura Corkery
TEXAS, USA

Sitting in the car during this cold grey day, I watch my son slowly hop out of the bus, dragging his Batman jacket behind him. I can tell something has happened. Without taking my eyes off him, I say to my daughter, "I think something's wrong with your brother." My daughter pipes up in her little pixie voice from the back of the car and, in her eight-year-old wisdom, says, "No, he looks fine to me."

As he walks slowly toward me, I can see the tears running down his face through the dust on the windshield. "No, he's crying. Something definitely happened," I say. I reach over to the car door while inwardly sighing. It's been a full day of work, and I know I have a busy night ahead of me.

I just got off a call with my husband. He had let me know on his way to work that our son's teacher called, and my son was in trouble at school again.

As I walk toward my son, I mentally shelve the conversation

I had planned to have with him. I feel the chill in the air as I reach out to give him a hug and rescue his Batman jacket from the ground. Before I can ask what happened, he says, "Two of the big boys on the bus cut in front of me and threw my tie into the back of the bus." I hold him close and look for the boys in question among the children milling around waiting to be picked up, mentally debating whether to ask them for their version of what happened. "They're brothers," he says.

"Okay, honey," I say as I wrestle with choosing between being the disciplinarian and taking care of my child, who is obviously hurting. "I'm sorry this happened. I know it must have hurt your feelings."

I sigh as I think about all the problems he's had with the "big boys" on the bus over the last few months, wishing that I could pick him up from school and avoid the issue altogether. I run through all the potential options again and come to the same conclusion. I can't be in two places at once. My daughter's school lets out at the same time as my son's, and it is in a completely different direction. My husband's schedule changed earlier this year, so he's not able to help with pickup. And we have already tried the after-care program at his school without any luck.

I look at his tear-stained face and say, "Would you like to go get a popsicle?" Although it is a brisk day, he immediately brightens, wipes the tears off his face, and climbs into the car. I give him an extra squeeze and brush a kiss on his cheek as I start buckling him into his car seat.

"Leila, we're going to get popsicles!" he calls out to his sister. The negotiating swiftly starts as they each throw out how many toppings they want to add. The merits of chocolate drizzle and cookie crumbles are being discussed in the back as I drive toward the nearest popsicle shop.

We pull into the parking lot, head inside, purchase our popsicles, and sit down to enjoy them. I focus on being fully present in the moment with my two beautiful babies and just having fun. As the kids discuss their flavor choices, I look around the brightly colored room decorated with large cutouts of popsicles painted red and yellow.

My heart swells at their sticky, smiling faces as I hope we are creating a wonderful memory that will lessen the sting of my son's experience on the bus today. We wrap up and head home to start the evening routine of dinner, making sure assignments are completed and getting everyone into bed before I can resume work.

After dinner, I settle into the couch, look at my five-year-old boy, and wonder how to start the conversation. "We got a call from your teacher, honey," I say.

"I know," he says, leaning up against the couch, not meeting my eyes. "She said she was going to call you."

We talk about what he's done, why it isn't okay, and how to make different choices the next time. As we close the conversation, I take a deep breath, and my mind starts to drift to the night ahead, getting the kids through their bedtime routine and the presentation I am working on for an upcoming speaking engagement.

"Mom," my son says slowly.

"Yeah, babe," I answer a little distractedly.

"I carry your heart in my head," he says. Stunned at what has just come out of my little boy's mouth, my attention snaps fully back on him. I take a breath, look at him, and ask him to repeat what he said, thinking I must have heard him wrong.

He repeats, "Mom, I carry your heart in my head."

As tears well up in my eyes, I ask, "What does that mean, honey?"

"I don't know," he says. "I just carry your heart in my head."

I look at my beautiful boy, and I let go of the need to analyze it. I surrender to the gift of the moment and say, "Okay, bud. I love you." I reach over to hug him, smelling his little boy smell, and I feel the soft brush of his hair on my cheek.

"Love you too, Mom."

A Change of Heart

Patricia Campbell
CANADA

I have always said I am a cat person, not a dog person. Both my beloved cats went to cat heaven, and I still miss having little fluff balls greet me at the door. My sister loves dogs. "Dogs are better," she often says. Perhaps there is a power to persuasion.

At some point, curiosity enters my mind. I start wondering, "What would it be like to have a dog?" I'm not serious, though, because everyone knows dogs tie you down, and I love to travel. It's one reason I love cats—they're so fabulously independent.

It's a beautiful July day, and I am at a yoga retreat in Nelson, B.C. I love Nelson, my birthplace, and I love yoga. It's a magical combination. This retreat is nine days long, and its focus is on healing. For me, it is about healing my inner child so I can be the woman I truly desire to be and live the life I dream of. It is deep and intense work at this retreat, and I am already feeling free and open-hearted.

Our final activity is to create a vision board using magazine pictures that call to us. There's no logical thinking or choosing after nine long days at a retreat filled with yoga, sharing, and talking. It's purely intuition at this point. Searching through the magazines, I find a picture of a group of white teddy bears, and I realize I never had a teddy bear as a child. This is a new awareness. I can't say I want a room full of white teddy bears, but somehow, I am drawn to this picture. It makes no sense because I don't want teddy bears. After all, I'm 64 years old, and it seems late for teddy bears.

Anyway, I'm not a teddy bear person. And yet, the picture calls to me with an energy I can't let go of. I cut it out and paste it on the board with the other images that I really want. They speak of more nature, more spiritual connection, and more love.

Home at last, I unpack and tuck the vision board away. It's time for a day of rest. And what better way to relax than opening up and reading the newspaper. Today, I look at the pet section, although I am not sure why. I chalk it up to missing my cats. Maybe it's the same reason I go on the Society for the Prevention of Cruelty to Animals (S.P.C.A.) website from time to time, to give myself a pet "fix." I often window-shop the S.P.C.A. sites like a pining teenager. Truly, I miss my cats. However, none of the cats on the website has called out to me.

But wait, there's an ad here in the newspaper. What's this? It's not clear. It's something about a family of little dogs. They are rescued dogs. They've been rescued from a puppy mill, and it's nearby. This ad speaks to me. They are gentle little dogs that were raised and kept in crates. They are being freed and need loving homes. So, I call the number. After all, it doesn't hurt to just get information. Maybe I can help them find a good home.

Something speaks to my heart from the information I gather. I drive two hours to meet the woman who rescued these four dogs.

Maybe, if it feels right, I can take one in, especially if it's a girl dog who is small and doesn't shed. I have these guidelines because, after all, I'm really a cat person. Everyone who knows me knows that.

It's a great day for a drive, and as I make my way to my destination, I see the blue van. I pull in and park. The woman who rescued the dogs opens the van's side door, and there's a little crate inside. She reaches in and brings out a trembling little ball of fur. I know instinctively I don't have what this little creature needs to take care of her. My heart is open, but it's not for her. I share, "I'm so sorry. She needs specialized care. Someone experienced."

But wait. "What's that rustling in the crate beside hers?" I have to see. The woman opens the crate, and another dirty ball of fluff peers out. I get closer, and this one reaches toward me and puts both front paws on my shoulders. He looks into my eyes and cuddles in. The woman says, "His name is Teddy Bear." Teddy Bear. A white teddy bear. Full of love to give and receive. My miracle dog. My dog. Now I can say I'm a dog person. For life.

The Big Move

Jackie Mieres-Johnston
CANADA

Another sleepless night in Trinidad! As I sit here having my coffee before heading out to work, I am wondering what other precautions we can take to keep our family safe in these times. Another business owner was kidnapped while he was on his way home from work. This is the third kidnapping this month.

As the country goes through an economic downturn, crime has been on the rise, and kidnappers are targeting business owners who they believe can pay a ransom. The crime situation is so bad that on one occasion, my husband was held up at gunpoint, and I know four people who have been murdered as a result of robberies.

My husband Terence and I have two beautiful children, a seven-year-old girl and a five-year-old boy. Terence is a business owner, and his office is located in a secluded area about an hour's drive from our home. We both know that we need to find a solution for the safety of our family.

Terence and I are sitting with the kids between us, and I feel a fluttering feeling in my stomach. I am dreading talking to my young children about kidnapping and how to stay safe. The kids understand what we are saying though, and now it's bedtime. So Terence takes them to their rooms to settle them in for the night.

Terence walks up to me in the kitchen, looks me straight in the eyes, and says, "I want to get a licensed gun. I will dismantle it when I get home and lock it away from the kids. I just want to feel safer."

"No, we will not have a gun in the house while we have young children," I respond.

It is now the middle of the night, and I am lying in bed staring at the ceiling. I'm filled with worry. What can I do to keep our family safe? Even if I agree to get a gun, that will not solve the problem. Maybe we could move to another country, but what would we be leaving behind? We were born here. Our families are here, and we love our jobs.

The children spend time with their cousins, and they enjoy playing with their friends. We love the warm weather and island life. I feel so at peace when I sit and experience the sunrise and sunset over the crystal-clear water. Listening to the birds in the trees and the waves. The feeling of the light breeze on my face. We would miss our friends and the extended family get-togethers. I will talk to Terence tomorrow about moving.

We talk, and we decide to move to Canada. To celebrate the move, we are all gathered on a boat that is heading to an island off of Trinidad to spend the weekend at our family cottage. The sky is a beautiful light blue with few clouds, and the sun's reflection on the water makes it look inviting to swim. I see something jumping out of the water in the distance.

As we move closer, I see it's a pod of dolphins! They come up to our boat, jumping out of the water and swimming along. They are so beautiful as they put on a show for us.

My husband stops the boat, and they swim around us and under the boat. We are so excited! The children and I rush to the side of the boat to look at these magnificent animals. One turns his head up and looks me straight in the eyes.

This special moment and connection give me a sense of peace that I can feel move through me. The sense that the future will be just as wondrous as this moment. As the dolphins drift away, Terence starts the boat, and we continue on our way towards the cottage.

Flash forward, I am sitting on board the plane to Canada in my upgraded business class seat. As I am waiting to take off, I am amazed at how everything with this move has worked out perfectly. I was able to keep my job, we were quickly accepted as permanent residents, and it only took one day to find a home with a five-minute walk to the children's school.

I finally feel relaxed with a sense of excitement in my heart. We are on our way. And we continue our journey, being guided by our Higher Power.

Truck Included

Katherine Loranger
CANADA

Pouring a glass of wine, I find myself drowning in a familiar sea of self-loathing, frustration, and despair. Wondering why I keep finding myself with partners where I feel unseen, unsupported, and unloved. Why am I feeling lonely and alone even while I am sitting right here beside someone I am committed to in our relationship? I notice the typical feelings I have. The feelings that my needs aren't important, or that it's even wrong or selfish for me to have needs or expectations of my partner. The pattern of entering a relationship and, after that, just making the best of it.

As I sit in front of the fireplace, watching the flames flicker and listening to the wind and rain of the storm, I begin to ask myself the same old questions. What's wrong with me? Why does this keep happening? Why won't someone love me? I have plenty of answers that come to mind, and when I look, I sure can find evidence to support these underlying beliefs. I feel like I am not good enough.

Sure, I've had moments or even stretches of time when I can remember experiencing some of the elements that I thought I wanted. But when I get right down to it, and if I am honest with myself, I don't actually even really know what I want and what is important to me. I've thought about it on a superficial level, but I haven't given myself the time to really create space for my heart and soul's deepest yearnings to reveal themselves to me.

I have been looking outside of myself for the answers, not really having a clear idea of what is important to me, and instead getting swept up in the thrill of something (or someone) new and different until I find myself in a committed long-term relationship just because it is what I thought is supposed to happen. Never even asking myself if it is truly what I want and truly who I want to be with.

As I feel myself slipping further into the familiar feelings of self-pity, something happens. Something different. I notice the well-worn path that my brain keeps taking me down. The path I nurse, rehearse, and reinforce. In this noticing, something shifts. A shift that is small and subtle, soft and gentle, yet powerful in its hopefulness.

I can bring to mind times in my life when I felt guided by something that I couldn't understand or even describe. Times when I've been in a consistent meditation practice, times in nature, and times when I felt connected to something bigger, wiser, and infinitely loving. And times when I just surrendered to the flow of life, and seemingly miraculous and unexplainable things happened.

I notice the familiar reaction and feelings, and at the same time, I am remembering these times in my life. I feel an opening within myself. It's cathartic, like the smell of fresh air after a violent storm paired with the sight of sunlight glistening on the beads of water dripping off the trees. A feeling of renewal. A feeling of possibility. A feeling of hope.

This openness causes me to ask different kinds of questions. What if what I want actually matters? What if I can have the kind of relationship that I dream of and what if I give myself permission to dream? What is important to me? What would I really love?

As these questions unfold, I take my pencil and a piece of paper and ask my heart and soul what is truly important to me when it comes to my relationships and my life. From these questions, a list emerges of qualities, character traits, emotional attributes, and a sense of adventure and fun. As I complete my list, I think to myself, *Let's add on there a big truck for gardening and home renovations.* And I let go . . .

A month later, I head over to Kenora, Ontario, to attend a friend's wedding. When he and his fiancée hear that I am single, they proceed to toss names back and forth to each other with the intent of setting me up. I laughingly tell them, "I am not interested in being set up, thank you very much."

They continue to suggest names to each other, with each name being dismissed by the other for various reasons. They are obviously having a lot of fun with it when all of a sudden, they stop, look at each other, and simultaneously say, "Robin." In spite of myself, I am intrigued, and they proceed to tell me that he is the kindest, most thoughtful, and the most upstanding man they had ever met. All qualities that I highly value.

They arrange for him to attend their pre-wedding BBQ so we can meet, but he doesn't show up. I shrug to myself and figure that it wasn't meant to be. Later, I find out that he'd driven by but was so nervous and shy because he didn't know anyone other than the bride and groom that he just kept driving.

Today is the big day! It's time for my friend's wedding ceremony, and it's being held at a different location than the reception. So they have a bus for transportation. As I board the bus, I immediately notice a handsome man with the most amazing smile. He glows with life and joy. He looks so alive and open to me.

As the bus arrives at the ceremony location, I find myself busy helping the party, and the man on the bus vanishes from my mind. During the reception, my friend comes over to me to tell me that he wants to introduce me to his friend Robin, the one that he and his fiancée had told me about. During the festivities, I had forgotten all about it, and when he introduces me, I see that it is the man I had noticed on the bus!

It turns out he had noticed me as well, and as I get to know him, he shares that he almost didn't attend the wedding at all because he'd gotten a call about a job just as he was about to board the bus. For some reason that he couldn't explain, he felt that he needed to turn it down and board the bus, and we are both so grateful that he did.

We both listened to the still, small voice inside us, and it brought us together. This wonderful man ends up becoming my husband. He embodies all of the qualities on my list, and he even has the big truck to boot!

Applied! Accepted! Now What?

Joan Luke

CALIFORNIA, USA

I enjoy the ideal high school life that most girls dream about. I am the class vice president, a four-year record-setting varsity letterman in track, and a varsity volleyball player. I am dating a celebrated star football player. I am an honors student, club president, publicity commissioner, and I have a lot of great friends. It's a dream. But as I near the end of my high school years, I wonder if the dream ends here.

Since my sophomore year, I have been dreaming about attending a top university. My deep yearning is to leave my hometown and expand my world and education by pursuing medicine, dentistry, or something better.

It's now the fall of my senior year, and my father was just laid off from work due to a recession. My mother is working a part-time job and selling real estate, but her income is not enough to support our family and my plans for a stellar college education. My mind is clear and focused as I continue to achieve top grades, all while I travel locally and visit potential universities.

Inspiration strikes! What if I join the road trip my friend is planning? He is visiting his brother at a distant college. So, I ask if I can tag along. His reply is, "Yes! If you can pitch in money for the gas." During the fall, we travel up to northern California to visit three of the top universities. A distance of 350 miles from home is as far as my teenage mind can allow me to consider living, learning, applying to, and possibly attending a university.

After six hours and a hurried fast-food break, we arrive at our stop—the first university. There are so many happy, laughing, and smiling faces everywhere. The weekend seems to be a huge success in gathering data for my mission of choosing a dream college. We make it to an epic college rivals' football game, go to a crowded beer-drinking frat party, eat typical college cafeteria food, visit and smell dorm rooms, and soak up as much information about the feel of each campus and what each has to offer. We enjoy a whirlwind college exploration at all three stops!

What are my findings? One university is way too big and requires taking up a social cause. I feel like I'd be swallowed up into the sea of students and never see my professor in a classroom until my junior year because the teachers' assistants teach the general education classes. Another campus, and its student body felt stuffy and overly interested in my social economic status, who my father is, and if he is of political significance or of great wealth.

The third university is not technically on my list. I have several friends attending this small private university. It's a quaint, lovely campus where people offer hellos while passing on the walkways between buildings, where professors know students by name, and where a focus and spirit of knowing an infinite source is celebrated. My heart and soul are singing, "This is it! This is where I'm going!" On the list, it goes!

Returning home, I get right to work so I can apply to the three universities. Sitting at my desk, head down, filling out my applications to my dream college, my father comes into my room. As he's looking over my shoulder, he says, "I don't know why you are applying to that school. I can't afford to send you to that school, even if I was working."

Turning my head, I look up and say, "If God wants me to be at that university, then I'll be at that university." As a young child, I had developed a strong intuition—an ability to listen and hear that powerful calm voice within me that gives me a "knowingness." It is all about a willingness to listen.

I have listened for this powerful, calm, and infinite inner voice so many times while looking for my direction. Should I try this sport? This instrument? This job? This class? The focus on this internal voice is reinforced by my daily practice of reading and reflecting on uplifting affirmations. A recurring theme for me is to let go and to let God. This is my life's anthem. All concern and worry dissolves at these words—let go, let God!

Joyfully, I receive letters of acceptance with financial aid packages from all three of the universities. Yet, my private university and top choice fell tens of thousands of dollars short of the cost of tuition, room, and board. Applied! Accepted! And not enough money for my dream college!

Two weeks before my high school graduation, the phone rings out of the blue, and I just know this is "the call." I restrain myself from answering the house telephone, and I listen, holding my breath as I watch my father answer. I stand frozen while listening to his staccato worded answers, "Hello, yes, yes, she has. Oh, really? Thank you. Okay, goodbye."

My eyes extend wide open. I ask, "What was that about?" My father looks at me dumbfounded and says, "That was the university. They told me about a person who would like to anonymously pay for your tuition, room, board, and books if you want to attend the private university." I explode, jumping and crying out loud. I knew it. I knew it! I knew it!!! It is surreal!

I attend that wonderful university along with several friends from my hometown. I am assigned a roommate who is from northern California. She is so beautiful, smart, and fun. I happily introduce her to my friends. She dates and, during our senior year, becomes engaged to one of my oldest friends from my hometown.

On college graduation day, we are all together at the ceremony with our families, and it is during this moment that my anonymous benefactor steps forward. He announces that he is the one responsible for the generous payments towards my four years of university education. I feel myself shake, and I have warm tears of love and gratitude flowing down my face. This man is the father of my hometown friend—the friend who I introduced to my roommate the first week of our freshman college year. It is such an unbelievable moment.

Two weeks later, we are all together again for their engagement party. When I enter the ballroom, my benefactor points at me and says, "You're the reason we are all here at this celebration! If I hadn't sent you to this school, I would never have had this beautiful daughter-in-law to-be!" His great, generous giving to me changed my life in every way and blessed him and his family abundantly.

Finding My Way Home

Tamara Wolfe
VIRGINIA, USA

"Stop!" This voice startles me as I get out of my car, and it brings me to tears. It seems to have come out of the blue, but I know that it has been whispering to me for some time, maybe even years. Today it is firm. It grabs my attention.

Fast forward a few months. I am in the emergency room waiting for the results from an abdominal CT scan while anxious and in pain. The doctor arrives with the news that my gall bladder is in bad shape and that I need to stay overnight for more testing. They also see a small mysterious mass on the scan as well. I am left feeling worried and anxious.

The next morning, I am greeted by an oncologist who wants to do blood work to screen for cancer. I cannot believe what I am hearing. My overnight stay turns into a three-day stay for more tests. I am shocked and scared. This cancer scare is magnified by my pastor's prayer visit and my adult son climbing onto my hospital bed to comfort me.

To my relief, I am clear of cancer, and I heed the recommendation to have my gall bladder removed. This health scare and the firm command from my inner voice are wake-up calls. Life is short, and it is time to explore what is on the other side of my longing and discontent. For my career, I am a leader in sales. Although I really love what I do, during the past few years, I have had a longing for something more. I am just not sure what that "more" is. And as a consequence, I feel myself losing sight of my life's vision. I feel stuck and out of alignment. Something has to change!

My career plateaus, and my discontent begins to spill over into other areas of my life. I feel like I am dying inside. I have been pushing this whisper down for years, thinking that there is no opportunity better than what I have. It's time to move from stop to start! I begin by looking past the good, and I start looking for the great.

One Saturday, my vision quest leads me to stumble across a mindset program while scrolling through social media. I can sense this program is going to be pivotal during my journey to the great. I am excited about the neuroscience aspect within it as well! I start teaching these concepts to my team to use in business.

One evening after a training, I realize I would love to teach this material to a larger audience. As I am doing an assessment as a part of this mindset program, one part stands out to me, clear as day. The curriculum says if I am not doing speaking engagements already, I should be.

Getting ready one morning, I watch an interview about my new mentor through this program. I am captivated by her story, and I know that I need to go to her upcoming event. It is no surprise that the theme of her event is discovering your vision. All sorts of things around me are beginning to align. I am so excited!

The minute I walk into the event, I feel at home. Coincidently, the event is held both in the city where my current business has its headquarters and in a hotel where they hold many of the company events.

At the opening reception, I am shocked to see a retired top leader from my company! I introduce myself, and she whispers in my ear, "Teach this to your people. This is what our company founder had taught us." I am not sure exactly what she means, but I am excited to find out! I feel like she is blessing my vision quest.

I feel like my two worlds are coming together as I step into the opening event. The atmosphere is familiar, filled with the excitement of music, dancing, inspiration, education, dreams being shared, and stories of transformation. I feel so alive and connected with this group of vision seekers! I realize that I am living out one of my hearts desires that I had expressed a year before—connecting with big thinkers and people who want to make a difference in the world! I am at home!

My vision becomes clear during the repeated partnering work throughout the weekend. I am passionate about helping others to discover their passion and purpose so that they can bring their gifts and talents to the world, and therefore, help others shine their lights as well. One of my partners tells me that she feels like I am already living the vision I am describing.

To my surprise, I discover that the institute sponsoring the conference is also offering a career opportunity. I am compelled to attend a lunch to hear more about this opportunity. As I am there listening to the speaker, I can't believe my ears. What they are describing is a perfect match to my newly discovered vision. I finally have a name for the career that I am seeking—transformational coach and speaker!

I think back to the networking events in recent years and how I had wished that my elevator pitch reflected something with a greater impact on people than what I was currently doing. I have found my calling! The puzzle pieces are all coming together.

My excitement is immediately met by voices saying, "You can't chase two rabbits," "You were going to be a lifer as a leader in your sales company," and "You don't have the money to invest." Feeling overwhelmed, I head back to my seat for the next session of the conference. Within a minute, my inner voice tells me, "Get up!" I literally feel like I am sprung out of my seat. I realize that it is scarier to leave the conference still feeling like I am dying inside than to listen to my heart and invest in this new opportunity. I choose to invest in my happiness!

My heart is racing after I make my investment, and as I muster up the words to tell my husband that I signed up to become a life coach. The years of being in limbo come rushing forward through my tears as I share my joy in connecting with what I would love for the next step in my life's journey to serve others. As I share this news, I suddenly remember that a year ago, my husband had suggested I should explore life coaching.

Although this career shift seems to come out of the blue, as I reflect, I am reminded of all the whispers and events along the way that led me to this moment. In an odd way, I am grateful for my health scare because it truly woke me up and moved me into action. I am also grateful for my intuition and my willingness to listen, even if I did not always know where it would take me. Each of these pieces of the puzzle are what led me to find my new home.

Great Is the Opposite of Good

Hailey Wong
CHINA

"I said you shouldn't use colorful rubber bands and to only use black ones for your hair. Can't you hear me?" says the teacher as she pulls my hair and twists my ear. This is how I get punished at school. And I not only get punished for what I wear in my hair, but I get in trouble for cheating and for my lies. I am so "naughty" as a seven-year-old girl.

After I get home, my parents find out I got punished at school, and they say, "Now you should stop crying when I beat you. Stop crying, and I stop beating." This is what I grow up knowing—being different has a cost. After all of this pain, I decide to become a good girl by working hard, listening, following, and getting good grades.

Things go smoothly up until it is time to apply for universities. While at school, my teacher tells me, "I don't think you should go to the university you mentioned. I think you might just be sitting there during the interview. There's no chance you can get in."

I ask, "Why?"

She says, "Your English is not good enough compared to the other candidates."

I am furious! I know I'm not good enough, but I don't know how to change that! Over the years, I am always working to be good, and now she says I am not good enough? Of course, I pass the interview and get in. Yet that experience keeps me wondering—how good is good enough?

The same realization about being good happens again as I get sick during my second year of college. My immune system is struggling. Before the illness, I used to go to bed and sleep for seven hours, eat fruits and vegetables, and swim three times a week. It turns out that is only good for the body, not for my inner self.

Sickness strikes me again during my first year as a teacher. I still have issues with my immune system, and I still don't understand why. I get rashes all over my legs, and I am confused. Luckily, the breakdown leads me to think about what these experiences and physical ailments are trying to tell me.

As I start to search within myself, I see the paradigms start to surface, such as "I am not good enough," "I am not worthy of success," and "I am afraid of not being the same as everybody else." I realize I have been ignoring the true, small voice that has been prompting me to make healthy changes and listen within myself, but I hadn't been paying attention to them. So, I have been suffering from not being obedient to what is seeking to emerge within.

Suddenly a realization comes to me—great is the opposite of good. I realize I am truly living when I am aware of what's happening and what's seeking to emerge. It's in the moment when I know I am awake to this; I become great. I am different, and I will never be the same as everybody else.

Today, as I am working on my dreams as a transformational life coach, I am happy and grateful that I choose to focus more on what's possible and how great I want to become in the process. "Follow your heart" is the still small voice that keeps reminding me to be great. If I want to have extraordinary results, I need to take extraordinary actions that lead to greatness.

The infinite has my back. And knowing that helps me turn from a good girl of the past to a great girl today, embracing her differences and believing in her dreams.

The Gain from the Loss

Aurelie Catherine Cormier
MASSACHUSETTS, USA

I am in the middle of my Sunday 12-hour shift on the oncology unit when I receive a call from my sister Maryellen. "I'm in the cardiac care unit (CCU) at your hospital where my husband's been admitted," she shares anxiously.

I ask, "What's going on?"

"It's hard to explain."

I reassure her. "I will be there shortly." I speak to the charge nurse and arrange to leave for the day.

Fifteen minutes later, I walk into the CCU in shock as I see my brother-in-law Bob lying in the hospital bed hooked up to a ventilator. Bob is a 53-year-old, active, humorous father, husband, and business owner. I talk with my sister to try to understand what happened.

Mary tells me, "Bob and his friends went down to Turks and Caicos for their annual guys' weekend. They had been out celebrating, and sometime during the evening, they got into a car accident. Bob was a passenger in the front seat and had hit his chest on the dashboard. After the accident, he was in considerable pain, so they decided to go to the hospital down there. It was late, so they dropped him off.

"While he was there, he was given IV pain medication. It didn't seem to be enough to take away the pain, so they gave him another dose. And not too long after that, he stopped breathing and didn't have oxygen for 25 minutes.

"By the time his friends got to the hospital in the morning, Bob was in a coma, so they had him med flighted to Massachusetts General Hospital in Boston." Mary is beyond distraught as she shares this with me.

Once he arrived here, Mary shares that the medical staff had started a therapeutic hypothermia process where his body temperature is lowered in an attempt to preserve brain function. I immediately realize the gravity of Bob's situation. This procedure can be successful if it's done within six hours of a code. In this case, it's after 18 hours. Despite these facts, the doctors and nursing staff are full throttle ahead and doing everything within their power to save Bob. My sister and I are beyond grateful.

I call the chaplain I often work with, and she arranges for the CCU chaplain to perform a prayer service for Bob while his friends and family are here. We need a miracle, and we all want to use this time to create the best environment for whatever is possible. It didn't take long for the priest to arrive. We all gather in a semi-circle around Bob's bed, holding hands for comfort. The priest leads the service, offering prayers, words of encouragement, and comfort.

At the end, he asks if we have any prayers we want to share.

I readily volunteer to share a heart-felt prayer along with Bob's friends and family members. In the middle of the prayer service, despite the fact that Bob is in a coma, a few large tears roll down the side of his face. My sister leans over and wipes them off. It is a powerful moment that speaks of the tenderness and care my sister has for her husband. It also confirms to me that Bob is truly present and is sensing everything that is happening. It's a sign that even while people are in a coma, they hear and are fully aware of our presence.

Two days later, Bob's temperature is brought back up to normal. Once his temperature is normalized, he is sent for a re-evaluation of his brain function. I have a set of prayer beads from Medjugorje, in Bosnia and Herzegovina, the site where the Blessed Mother is said to have appeared to six young children in 1981. I ask my sister if I can bring them in and put them on Bob's wrist. My sister says yes. So, I get the prayer beads and wrap them around his right wrist.

It's a time when it's quieter in the room, and I am able to spend some time talking to Bob. I let him know how sorry I feel that he is in this situation and that this is happening to him. I let him know what a wonderful father he is to his daughters, Abbie and Sadie, and how much we all enjoy his Thanksgiving dinners that he cooks every year for the family.

The next day, the tests come back. It's what we have feared. Bob has moderate to severe brain damage from the hypoxia experienced during the code. The doctors relay that this is a grave sign. My sister realizes the implications.

The New England Organ Bank wants to discuss the options with my sister, so we have a meeting where they can review what the options are. Their liaison is sensitive to what a difficult decision this is and how stressful this is for my sister, and they are immensely informative, understanding, and caring.

My sister handles this intense time with such grace. She knows that Bob has always expressed a desire to donate his organs, if at all possible. We listen, and she does exactly as Bob would have wanted. She decides to donate as many organs as possible, which means they will need to wait until he is officially brain dead before they can bring him to the operating room, and while he is still ventilated, procure his organs. This is a difficult decision for my sister, but it's an expression of carrying out what Bob would want.

The next morning, I wake up early. I head into my kitchen and look out the window, and something catches my attention. A solar light atop the gate is blinking to the rhythm of a heartbeat. I have never seen this happen with these solar lights before! I immediately know it's a message. Without hesitation, I call my sister and tell her what is happening.

That same afternoon, my sister gets a call from the New England Organ Donor Bank that Bob's heart is being donated. It is a day we will never forget. My sister is in shock, and yet she is able to hold it together enough to make arrangements for the funeral mass and funeral.

A few weeks pass by, and we are still readjusting to the recent events. As an oncology nurse/nurse practitioner, I have learned so well from my patients that while we can never understand why challenging experiences occur, there is always something positive that we can glean from them. I know that at some point, a positive message will come.

A few weeks later, in the middle of the night, as I am sleeping, I feel something gently scratching my right wrist. At first, it scares me, so I quickly pull my arm under the covers. What was that? All of a sudden, it comes to me. That is where I had placed the beads on Bob's wrist to give him strength. He is thanking me for the Medjugorje rosary beads. I now know he is at peace!

Within a year, my sister discovers that ninety people are recipients of either his organs, bones, or skin. This is the positive message we need. Through Bob's life and generosity, he has positively made a difference in the lives of ninety people!

The Price of Admission

Dawn M. Zehren

WISCONSIN, USA

Suddenly I realize and exclaim, "I don't have my driver's license with me!"

My husband's face goes blank, "You sure?"

"Yep," I reply at a loss.

My husband Nick looks around, trying to figure out what to do. There is only one exit left before the expressway to the airport.

"Should I get off here and turn around? Do we have enough time to get your license and still make the flight?" he asks.

"Nope," I reply. "There's not enough time."

After a moment of thought, my husband shares, "I'm still going to turn around to go home. Even if you can reschedule for a later flight, you will still need your license."

"Nope," I say again. "We are almost to the airport. Drop me off like normal. I am getting on my flight." To my delight, I'm not worried about it. I'm not angry at myself. I'm not even disappointed.

Yes. I am without my driver's license. Yes. Government-issued photo I.D. is required to board flights. No. I don't know how I will get on my flight. Still, I am calm and certain it will work out.

Nick doesn't ask too many more questions because he is devising how to best support me. While Nick doesn't believe I will be allowed to fly, he can easily see that I believe.

He drops me off but isn't going home. Instead, he parks the car and meets me inside. "Just in case." I sift through things to get my boarding pass while I greet the airline counter attendant as I do most clerks, servers, and most anyone who helps me. I ask their names, introduce myself, and thank them for their help. I love witnessing people shift when they realize someone actually sees them as a person and acknowledges their service.

The attendant smiles. Then, I tell him I have a problem. "I don't have my driver's license with me. I have my flight info, and I have the charge card I bought my ticket with, just no license. Would it be okay to get on the flight anyway?" I ask. "After all, I'm not the one driving."

Thankfully, he laughs at my humor. "We don't have a problem with you boarding the flight," he says, "but I am not sure that TSA will feel the same way." He checks his watch and tells me to get to TSA right away. Walking over, I see Nick is waiting at the TSA line. He isn't able to go in line without a boarding pass, but he is allowed to walk next to it to hear the outcome.

I approach the TSA officer with the same gratitude I have for the airline attendant. He smiles too. I tell him I have a problem, and his look changes as if to say, "Oh really? What now?" I let him know. "The problem is mine, and I am the only one responsible." His face softens. I share, "I believe you will be able to help me, but if you aren't able to, I understand. Again, I am the one responsible." With that, he asks how he can help.

"My driver's license is on my kitchen table," I explain. "The airline issued my boarding pass and is okay with me flying. I have credit cards with my name on them. Does it help at all that my business cards have my photo on them?" He chuckles and looks everything over.

He asks me a few questions and clears me to fly but says I better get my license to San Diego if I want to make my return flight home. I thank him, and I tell him my husband will overnight the license as I point to Nick. The TSA officer waives to Nick and gives him a thumbs up. Nick returns the gesture with a big smile. I can tell he hardly believes I am on my way.

The flight is delightful. I am floating in a sea of gratitude. I am grateful for the safe flight, the passengers around me, the flight crew, the counter attendant, and the TSA officer. I am grateful for Nick's willingness to allow me to act as if everything will work out, even if he didn't believe it himself.

I am grateful for the forty-eight hours I have in San Diego. Yep. That's it. Forty-eight hours. A quick trip for a special one-day workshop on a Saturday. Every three months, fifty sales professionals meet to expand their businesses and lives. I have been loving these trips and people from the very start. I typically fly in on a Friday and leave early Sunday. Traveling on a shoestring budget, I skip staying at the oceanfront hotel and restaurants. I stay inland and solo at my sister-in-law's condo; what a gift! Rental cars and groceries are so much cheaper. This is how I make it work while growing my business.

This is my fourth trip, and I have an established rhythm. But leaving my license on the kitchen table changes everything. While I have been allowed to fly, I am not able to rent a car like usual, and I accept the situation. My transportation options are walking or taking a cab. And as this sinks in, I start to feel let down.

In my short trips, I still make time to go out and explore. Downtown is alive with shops and people. The ocean offers the sound of waves, the warmth of sand, and spectacular views of sunsets. Balboa Park is a collection of jewels—gardens, museums, theatres, shops, and so, so much more. With a limited budget for cab fare, I feel like a great adventure is out of reach this time around.

I start to feel sad. And as I notice my shifting mood, it gets my attention. So far, I have spent my day in the center stream of abundance, regardless of my conditions. The results are astounding. I am so "in the flow" that I achieved what others wouldn't dare to attempt. Being in the flow feels fantastic. I decide now is not the time to leave this stream. So, I head out for adventure.

Walking, I feel the warmth of the sun on my face. I thank my strong, capable body. I inhale deeply and take in the view of the homes and gardens that are so different from mine in Milwaukee, Wisconsin. The world seems to shine.

I find nifty shops, each with charming clerks and owners happy to talk. In an eclectic resale shop, I discover treasures to take home. The shop owner lets me know that these items all belonged to the same woman. I wonder about this woman I will never meet. What is her story? We like the same items. What else do we have in common?

My evening is as glorious as my morning. The next two days deliver an even greater good with life-changing experiences and people I'll never forget. All of this and more was mine to access.

When people ask me how I made it on a plane without my license, I tell them, "I didn't do it alone, yet no one did it for me."

I find the price of admission to a first-class weekend so affordable. It turns out the secret is the rate of exchange. When I exchange everything else for gratitude, I realize and welcome all of my desires. And more.

Given Strength to Stop

Chris Barber

CALIFORNIA, USA

It's Monday, and my husband and I are returning home from a long weekend in Palm Springs, California. Sounds lovely, right? Well, it was, except it entailed another drinking binge. I spent way more money than I had, and worst of all, I knew I had embarrassed both of us. In all honesty, I don't remember chunks of time from this past weekend. It's a terrible feeling. A feeling I am all too familiar with.

After we get home, I am in front of the closet, putting away our clothes from the trip. I feel physically terrible and emotionally disconnected from my husband. I feel ashamed and deeply sad about how my drinking and my behavior had spoiled any good parts of the trip.

Have you ever felt stuck? Like you know that you want a different outcome in life, but you keep repeating the same patterns. And you know that there is more for you, but you can't see how to get there. Well, that's me.

Still standing in front of my closet, I suddenly hear a voice from inside of me saying, "Maybe you don't need to do that anymore." This is not at all the voice of my usual peanut gallery—the voice that always scolds me or tries to justify my behavior. This voice is different. My first response is laughter, and I think, *Yah, right, there's no way I can stop.* I know intimately about my lengthy relationship with addiction.

The energy or feeling of this voice and these words linger, and they are almost like a hand extending towards me to lead me to a path. But I have to decide. Maybe I can change. And with this little bit of hope and light ahead of me, I make a decision to stop drinking. And to take it one day at a time. I think about it, and I am not sharing this decision with my husband because he has heard me say I should stop drinking so many times before.

This new me is requiring me to get comfortable with being uncomfortable for a period of time. At first, it is extremely awkward and unfamiliar. I have never been here before with this mindset. First, it's days, then weeks, then months, and over time, the uncomfortableness fades away. As I become clearer, I begin to notice a common thread that weaves throughout my entire life—I have always loved transformation.

As a hairdresser, I help people physically transform. I also connect with them on a real and heartfelt level. My clients often tell me, "This is so much more than a haircut. I feel like I am coming away with a new perspective."

Still alcohol-free, it's been two years since that life-changing day back in 2015. It's Friday, the salon is buzzing, and I am with one of my favorite clients at the salon. She is telling me about a friend of hers who just returned from the most amazing weekend. My client is so happy for her friend, and you can sense the excitement.

My client goes on to say, "I feel like I am meant to tell you about this." She fills me in on a transformational life coaching program and about the founder who led the conference.

Up until this point, the only life coach I have known is someone who took advantage of some dear friends of ours, so I didn't light up right away. We connect on a deeper level, and this had something to it. I went on with my day, and something wouldn't leave me alone about it, though, so I say, "If this is for me, give me a sign."

Going through the rest of my day, I receive sign after sign. Finally, I go online to the site that points me in the direction to learn more about this life coaching company. I end up jumping on the phone with an enrollment specialist, and it is like magic. I feel like I am having a soul conversation. I feel immediate electricity. This is for me! This is me!

The certification process is rigorous and is quite an investment of time and money. But this time, I am "spending money" on something that will last and have an impact on my life and on the lives of others. Coaching is all about transformation—transformation on the inside so that people can connect to what really makes them happy and live a life they love.

I have always loved helping people feel better as far back as I can remember. Even in my worst stages of addiction. Today I am sober, I am present, and I get to help people transform on a much deeper level with life-giving lasting results. I am so happy and grateful I listened to that voice and made a decision.

Break Down to Break Through

Meredith Morse

COLORADO, USA

Feeling raw and shattered, I sit slumped over my desk, trying to hide my puffy, red eyes and tear-stained cheeks. The same question is stuck on replay in my head. "How could he marry another woman only one month after we break up?!"

Riddled with confusion and devastation, I struggle to keep a grip mentally. "WE had been the ones talking about marriage!" I scream internally. I try to fight back the tears, but the growing anger is overwhelming. I can't hold back any longer. Nausea consumes me while my whole body shakes as I try to maintain composure.

I feel wounded—slowly dying inside. Suffocating from the windowless concrete walls that surround me, struggling to find meaning in an unfulfilling job, beating myself up for all of my relationship failures, I weep again. I have no idea where to go or what my purpose is anymore. I am completely broken.

"What is so wrong with me that I can never get a relationship right?" I think silently as the tears continue flowing and a deep ache pounds within my chest. I am stuck in darkness and can't see my way out of the pain. My soul is broken. I have had enough and desperately want to escape my life.

I silently pray, "Please . . . please just give me a sign. I can't do this anymore. I don't want to hurt anymore. Please help me." As I begin to wipe my tears and pull myself together, an email appears in my inbox. As I scan it, I see it's an invitation to join a group life coaching program.

"What the heck is this?" I am not in the mood for a cheerleader squad. Doubt and hesitation creep in. I am not sure what this is all about, but I continue to read on. It seems like something that can help. But am I ready for something like this? Can I afford it?

Suddenly, a still, small voice emerges from deep inside, saying, "Yes! THIS is your sign! THIS is your chance to rise from the darkness and change your life." And in this moment, I decide. I click the button, quickly enter my credit card numbers, and enroll before any other doubts can creep in and dissuade me. I decide to break free and take a step towards a new life instead of staying stuck in doubt, fear, and misery.

This is MY time. For a long time, I have been devoting my life to men who never treat me right. I've let them call the shots so I didn't have to make any decisions. It is way easier to focus on them instead of fixing me. But no longer. I decide it is time to love and honor myself. I devote my time and energy to my personal coaching and uncover who I truly am and how to love myself fully and deeply—without anyone else's permission.

After studying and applying the principles of transformation, within months, profound shifts begin to take place. I adopt the type of dog I have always wanted, I land a promotion, and I move to the mountains where life is much brighter.

Although many things change externally, I feel the greatest shift come from within. I am stronger, more confident, and no longer need validation from a man to feel I am worth something. I discover who I truly am and what my soul's purpose is. I am free. My soul smiles. I walk in nature, turning my face to the sunshine and smiling as I feel its warmth. I know that I'm on a beautiful journey of becoming who I was always meant to be. I had to break down in order to break through. It took meeting my darkest hour before I could see my own glowing light from within.

Dog Person

Didi Selwa
CALIFORNIA, USA

It's a beautiful Southern California day. I feel the warm sun on my skin and smell the crisp, fresh air. My friend Sam and I are strolling along the walkway by the beach. As I am admiring this gorgeous ocean view and the people enjoying the beach, I hear Sam call out, "Oh, look at the doggie!"

I glance down and see a little wiener dog. Sam is completely mesmerized. She's petting and talking sweetly to the dog. She asks the owner, "What's its name?" Fortunately, my oversized sunglasses conceal my eye roll.

"Didi, isn't she cute!" she exclaims.

"Yeah, she is," I respond with a slight smirk. Meanwhile, I am thinking *Big whoop*! I am not really a dog person. They are cute, sure. And I know most people love dogs, especially where I live, but it's just not my thing.

As we walk away, Sam says, "I wish I could have a dog."

"Seems like a lot of work," I respond.

Several weeks later, I find myself watching the movie *A Dog's Purpose*. And surprisingly, I love the movie! Even more surprising, I hear a little voice say, "Get a dog." I dismiss this idea because, like I said, I am not a dog person.

Over the next few months, I keep having the same voice coming back and telling me to "Get a dog." And I can't believe this! Why do I keep getting this message? I have never been a dog person. After a while though, I start entertaining the idea of getting a dog. I am not sure how to process this, and I don't know what to do. So, I decide to make a pros and cons list. The pros list is simple. Dogs are cute.

The cons list includes that I have to walk it every day, even when I don't feel like it, even when I'm sick, and even if it's raining. I mean, these Southern California winters are brutal, right? Don't even get me started on potty training! I have been there and done that with my son. The dog will ruin my stuff. What if it chews up my beautiful shoes?! Ugh, the horror! And lastly, I'm not a dog person.

Forget it. I can't get a dog! But there is that voice prompting me again, that still, small voice saying, "Get a dog." Fine! All of the reasons for not getting a dog are completely valid, but I know I am getting this message for a reason. Okay, I am doing this. I tell my friends and family about my decision. "I am getting a dog." I never thought I would say these words.

My search for a dog begins. I start checking out puppies for adoption on different websites. As I am scrolling through, I spot a really cute one! She's not too big, not too small, and short hair—looks like a winner! I call to find out how I can adopt her, and the agency tells me, "She's already been adopted." I accept the answer and continue my search. But this keeps happening over and over again. Maybe I should give up. I mean, hey, I tried! I will give it a couple more weeks, but if it doesn't happen by then, then it's not meant to be.

My search online continues, and I spot a cute puppy that is ready to be adopted! A boy with golden fur, green eyes, and the hugest ears I've ever seen. I call the rescue, unsure if I am too late again. "Is Shy Guy still available?" I ask.

"He is still here and ready for adoption," they reply. I drive over to the rescue shelter. I am excited and nervous to meet him! The minute I see him playing with his brother in the pen, I know that Shy Guy is my guy.

A million potty "accidents" later, a few chewed up bathmats, one destroyed credit card (not mine), many thoughts of "Why did I do this?" and a few bites out of a flip flop later, Ty, formerly Shy Guy, not only rules the roost, but he rules my heart.

Day by day, he works his way into my soul. When I come home from work, he is there to greet me, running towards me and jumping on me. As I bend down, he wraps his little paws around my neck in an embrace. I don't know anyone who's ever been this thrilled to see me!

He's very rambunctious and gets excited when family and friends come to visit. Ty runs around the room in circles, as fast as he can, jumping on the couch and all over me as I sit and laugh. If he really likes someone, he might even tinkle on their feet in sheer delight. It's his way of baptizing them into his pack.

Ty's my fierce protector, barking at anyone who even drives slowly by the house. But once he settles down, he cuddles next to me and burrows under the covers. More than anything, though, I love the way in which he loves. His love is blatantly unconditional and unabashedly affectionate. I admire that and strive to love like he does.

It's time for our walk. I grab my black and white baseball cap with the words 'Dog Person' on it. I proudly wear this like a badge of honor. As we step outside, I look at this wonderful being who is such a big part of my life, and this dog mom has paws forever imprinted on her heart.

I am glad I listened to that still, small voice. He's not only changed who I am but who I perceive myself to be. He opens my heart and gives me more joy, laughter, and love than I could have imagined. He's made me a dog person, or at least this dog's person.

Dream Building from the Rubble

Karoline Stevens

ARIZONA, USA

I gaze out the window at the picturesque view across the estuary from my home, marveling at the snow-capped mountains in the distance. New Zealand is a jewel of the South Pacific, known worldwide for its pristine blue waters, rugged mountains, and vivid green pastures that stretch across its countryside. It's an idyllic place for hikers, surfers, adventure-seekers, and my family.

Lately, things have begun to crash down. My relationship ended, my business is lagging, and I can feel a growing restlessness churning inside of me. Deep down, I sense that change is in the air.

As I think about this, I suddenly feel something underfoot. Sometimes life's cosmic wakeup calls come in subtle signs. A nudge, a tap on the shoulder, or synchronicities. For me, the final wakeup arrives in the form of one of New Zealand's most devastating earthquakes, and I am finding myself at its epicenter!

Without warning, an ominous rumbling sound grabs the

attention of my mom and me as we are going about our daily business. Suddenly, our home is shaking violently from side to side. It's
as if a sleeping dragon is being angrily awakened and roaring to
life right beneath our feet.

These are ten of the longest seconds of my life! My focus is
fully on my mom, who is clenching onto an ironing board to keep
from falling. I am trying desperately to reach her, but I can't let
go of the kitchen counter without my feet giving way underneath.

My home, my family, and my entire world are suddenly being
shaken at its core. I have complete tunnel vision on my mother
and her safety to the extent that I barely process the sound of
dishes crashing to the floor from the cabinets. The bookshelves
are toppling over, tossing collections of treasures across the room.
I don't even notice the mess of food and containers sliding out of
the refrigerator as this massive machine starts to lose its footing.

Suddenly, everything is still. To my relief, my mom is okay.
Instinctively, we race out of the house with only one thing on our
minds. My son. Is he okay? How long will it be before we know?
Without internet or cell service, we finally receive word that he is
safe.

As we gather together in our mess of a home, we pop the cork
on a bottle of bubbly and open a package of smoked salmon that
has miraculously survived. We share a special moment and a drink.
We are disheveled and in shock but also grateful that our family
is safe. We soon discover that eleven of my friends are among the
185 people who are not so fortunate.

This event is literally an earthshaking end to a significant
chapter of my life. Despite the upheaval, I already feel encouraged
by a vision of something better to come. A life I know I will love!
And I am holding onto glimpses of how it might look as I think

back to my thoughtfully and purposefully created vision board from a while ago.

I look forward longingly to the wonderful life I am imagining. An amazing relationship with my soul companion, living in a beautiful home, leading a fulfilling and prosperous business, and having enriching experiences through travel. It's all right here in front of me. Where it takes place, however, remains a mystery. The answer may reveal itself to be one of several places. Possibly right here in New Zealand. Or maybe I'll move to Australia and search for it there. Or perhaps I'll be more nomadic and travel. Travel. What an alluring ring that word has.

Up until now, I have been used to a lot of structure in my life. Before today, I knew exactly when and what to do as a control freak in recovery. Now here I stand, my world has come crashing down around me, and I am facing the unknown with nothing to hold on to but a dream and a vision while freefalling.

A reassuring quote comes to my mind. "When you come to the edge of all that you know, you must believe in one of two things: that you will be given earth upon which to stand, or you will be given wings." This experience has certainly shown me I can't always count on the earth under my feet to be steady. It's time to fly. But where to?

While mulling this over with a friend in the United States, she mentions a healer she knows near Sedona, Arizona—a place known for world-class spas, intuitive healers, and Native American mysticism. Perhaps, she suggests, I can start there. I think back to my visit to Sedona ten years ago and how I had quickly fallen in love with it. This piques my interest.

Healing. Yes, there is so much to heal from. A healing trip is just what the doctor ordered. From a more whole place, I hope, from there I can decide my next move. I may not know it consciously yet, but I have a feeling Sedona has more in store for me than a simple stopover.

Little by little, as I relax into the unknown and let go of needing to be in control, the most amazing things begin to happen. Life begins to roll out the red carpet for me, and things are put in my path with the most synchronistic timing: places to stay, exciting invitations, and doors to new opportunities opening just as I am ready to walk through them. Friends are even noticing and commenting on how I am changing.

It's also amazing what happens. I suddenly realize that when I stop trying to control my life, that is when I find myself aligned with its flow. The flow we are all invited to be in. And because I believe the universe likes to sprinkle a little pixie dust on our path to let us know we're on the right one, I also begin to see more and more things on my vision board unfolding.

I meet my soul mate, who is an amazing, fun, and loving man who becomes my husband a year later. We have a beautiful home in the enchanted red rock country of Sedona. On top of this, my business is flourishing. Like a phoenix rising from a far-away earthquake, my story has become an inspiration for others who are ready to build a dream of their own.

The Sacred Gift of Life's Challenges

Martha Grier

NEW YORK, USA

My body is on fire. What started as an occasional itch is now incessant torture. The antihistamine my doctor prescribed isn't working. I retreat from life. All I can manage to do is go to work and come home. I am out of my mind as my body takes center stage. Something's got to give. Deep down, I know that I need to be still. I need to stop taking care of everyone else before taking care of myself. I need to stop running from one experience to the next, one relationship to the next, with no purposeful direction or meaningful desire. Maybe it's time for a getaway so I can sort things out.

One dry outfit. One wet outfit. Clothes to sleep in. Those are the instructions I receive in preparation to travel the Napo river to the site where I'll spend the next five days in the jungle. My group arrives in Quito a few days before the official excursion.

We make our way south to Tena—acclimating to the altitude and learning about Ecuadorian culture. The pace of life has a rhythm that is easy and embracing. The warmth of the people and the weather is welcoming, lush, and relaxing. It's a stark contrast to snowy Boston where I live a super-busy life as an entrepreneur.

Busy is my drug of choice, and it has been for decades. I'm not on this shamanic healing trip because I'm interested in becoming a shamanic healer. I need a vacation from my relationship and hectic life.

Swoosh . . . Swoosh . . . Swoosh. The sound of the oars in and out of the water as we ride in the longboats on the river makes it feel like I'm in a National Geographic documentary. I know why the color of the heart chakra is green. Seeing and feeling the greenery, buoyed by the flow of the water, feels like a dream. The boats pull over, and we disembark to hike several hours to the ecolodge.

Before leaving Boston, I vowed to stay open to every experience. I didn't want fear to get in the way of enjoying this once-in-a-lifetime opportunity. I also have a sense that there's something I need to let go of and am open to discovering what it is.

The hike is hot, humid, and exhausting. Taking one step at a time, we walk as fast as the slowest walker. Walking the narrow, sometimes precarious path created by previous explorers, I have to be mindful of where I place my hands and feet because touching a tree to steady myself could lead to being bitten by jungle creepy-crawlies. I notice that the road less traveled isn't as muddy. By the time we arrive at the compound several hours later, the jungle feels like home to me.

My vow to overcome fear is tested the very next day as the group hikes to a waterfall. What I think is going to be an interesting excursion there and back turns out to be me coming face-to-face with a fear I don't even know I have.

The hike is interesting. We learn about the "soap plant" that has leaves that release a soap-like substance when macerated. We learn how delicious lemon ants are and how they are also a good bug repellent when crushed and rubbed on the body. I also learn that I am terrified of walking across a fallen tree suspended over raging rapids with only a rope to hold onto.

No way, not doing it is my immediate reaction. My heart races, and my stomach flips. I'm terrified and, for a split second, consider turning back. Our Ecuadorian guide, Juan, graciously offers to accompany me across. With him by my side, looking down at my feet, holding onto the rope for dear life, and taking the smallest baby steps EVER, I do it! It is exhilarating to face fear head-on. I learn that taking even the smallest step, with assistance if needed, will eventually get me to where I need to go.

On our third night there, while trying to meditate and hold space for members of our group who are doing ceremony, I spontaneously leave my body. One moment, I'm there, and the next, I'm gone. I can't tell where my physical body begins or ends. Waves of bliss are coursing through my Being. I feel like I'm One with the universe. I'm the sounds of the jungle and the light of all that is.

Juan comes around to check on us. He sees a white light coming straight down into my body. He fetches the trip leader Dolores. At some point, she walks me to Don Augustin so that he can perform a clearing ritual on me. I am still blissing out. The experience lasts for about three hours. Little do I know, I'm cured of two chronic health conditions and have become gifted with the ability to access the non-physical side of life and heal others.

The trip that is supposed to be a vacation from my boyfriend instead ends up becoming a miracle. My intention to let go of what no longer serves me is paying off. I begin to release my history of childhood sexual abuse, domestic violence, and putting others' needs before my own. This release brings healing in a way that is similar to my cured chronic illnesses, and it provides me with refreshed direction and purpose. I am now initiated into my next level of personal power.

Among all the many lessons I learn, the most important one is that love is the energy that runs this whole show. No matter what life looks like on the surface, there's something seeking to be healed underneath. When I set an intention, release resistance, and surrender my fear and "less-than" feelings, life can change on a dime.

Knowing that life isn't just what I can see and feel is empowering. Sometimes taking baby steps, I allow my sense of trust to influence my choices. I know that challenges are presented when it's time to up-level. There's no reason for me to fear them though, because they are opportunities for deepening spiritual connection and authenticity.

After mistrusting people and feeling alone for most of my life, I take comfort in the fact that helpers and guides are all around. When I seek, I find. When I ask, I receive. When I'm still, I know. When I'm love, I'm free.

By the Light, I See

Amy Beth Kauffman
NEW YORK, USA

The sun is setting as I spread out the tablecloth. I place the candlesticks on the table and then add the white candles to the holders. I know exactly what I plan to say once the candles are lit. I gave it a lot of consideration during the week, and I made up my mind. I have no idea if my words will make a difference, but I have decided it is important enough to give my full attention and effort.

For years, I watched with wonder while my mom lit candles on Friday nights. I stood next to her in silent admiration while watching her wave her hands over the flames before covering her eyes. Her lips would move in silent prayer. It seemed to be an intensely personal and powerful moment, which often brought tears to her eyes. I wondered what she said and heard in her silent moment. I was so intrigued that I decided to light candles on Friday nights too. I paused to consider what my silent prayers will be. What do I want? I am thirteen years old, and I have everything I can imagine.

It is the '70s, and I am the oldest of three children living with my family in Princeton Junction, a suburb in central New Jersey. This once farming town is now being parceled out for new single-family home construction. We are four miles from Princeton and the home of the Ivy League university, 40 miles from the shoreline, and 55 miles from the Manhattan skyscrapers.

The yards of the new homes are sparsely dotted with young tree saplings, so our lawns grow unobstructed and with each yard rolling into the next. There are no fences, no locked houses, and no cell phones. On any given day, I wander out the back door of my house into our spacious backyard, and I listen for the sound of neighborhood friends to play with. We swing from playground monkey bars, jump rope, play kickball, ride bikes, catch fireflies, have snowball fights, and so much more! We roam from yard to yard playing outside all day. It is fun!

I enjoy staying awake to watch Jerry Lewis's annual Labor Day telethon, where he performs on stage all night. This is to raise funds for Muscular Dystrophy, a genetic disease that causes progressive weakness and loss of muscle mass. This telethon is my first broad exposure to people suffering with a chronic illness. It touches my heart.

Though I am only thirteen, that telethon raises my awareness and appreciation of my own physical abilities. I can see the birds in the trees, the smile on my mom's lips. I can hear the cars on the road, smell the blooming flowers, and gaze at the stars in the night sky. I am more appreciative of my ability to walk, run, and jump. I know how fortunate I am.

Mrs. F. is a wife and mom in the neighborhood who lost her eyesight to Multiple Sclerosis, an auto-immune disease affecting the protective covering of the nerves. It breaks my heart that she can no longer see her two daughters. Her older daughter is a few years shy of graduating high school, and I want her to be able to see her daughter walk across the stage in a cap and gown, to see her shake hands with the principal and superintendent. I want her to be able to see her daughter's smile and read her name on the diploma.

I don't know Mrs. F. well. Her older daughter is two years older than me, and her younger daughter is one year younger. Although we live around the corner, neither my parents nor I have daily contact with the family. Still, I feel sad about their situation.

After deliberating about what I want to say in my silent moment this Friday night, I decide that what I want most is for Mrs. F. to regain her vision. I am a little nervous, having never before asked for something in this manner, and certainly not of this magnitude.

While standing beside the table with the flames of the Friday night candles flickering, I close my eyes. I breathe in the significance of the moment and whisper the words in my heart: *Please let Mrs. F. see again.* It is an emotional and empowering moment for me. I can feel the energy shift in and around me. A lump forms in my throat, and tears fill my eyes. In those few minutes, I can feel myself grow in a deep and profound way. I know I will never be the same.

Week after week, I light the candles with joy and faith. I recite the words that Mom is teaching me to say while drawing the light towards me. I recite the traditional blessing of gratitude for being able to light the candles. And then, with my eyes closed, I silently express my deepest desire: *Please let Mrs. F. see again.* I wordlessly speak of my longing for her to regain her eyesight. For her to be able to see her daughter graduate and to behold the beauty of her family and her surroundings with her own eyes. I am very clear and very consistent: *Please, let Mrs. F. see again.*

I have no idea how it could happen, yet I believe that there is power and possibility in my thinking. I want this more than anything. I confidently hold tight to the image of it being true. I envision Mrs. F. seeing her daughter wearing the cap and gown. I envision her seeing the sunshine and glory of graduation day. And I am steadfast when I light candles each week. I love the hopeful and energized feeling I have in my soul doing it.

One afternoon, the phone rings unexpectedly, and I see my mother's expression shift from shock to tears. She hangs up the receiver and tells me that something happened to Mrs. F earlier today. Mrs. F. stepped into the shower, and suddenly, she saw the water!

Mrs. F. can see the water!!! Mrs. F. can see!!! And as sure as I know my name, I know that I played a part in making it happen. I am moved to tears. My heart feels full. After years of blindness, Mrs. F. regains her vision and sees her daughter graduate. Both daughters, in fact! She still has her eyesight today, more than 35 years later.

I have always felt connected to the energy of the universe— connected to a force greater than myself. As a teenager, I understood deeply that I am able to create incredible things using the power of my own thinking. With faith and clarity, I experience powerful results, even in holding the space for someone else's greatness. This awareness continues to fuel my hope and drive every single day. I am grateful for all that I have, all that I am, and all that I can do. I proudly light candles on Friday nights. And by the light, I see all that is possible.

I Would Have Saved
My Marriage

Raquel Hernandez-Meyer

CALIFORNIA, USA

It's Thursday morning as I receive my husband's text, "My father passed." Time suddenly freezes. I can feel my breathing getting shallow and my hands clammy. During this eternal moment, I stand up and go straight to the Human Resources manager's office. I stand at her doorway looking way past her, my hands are trembling, and I hear myself say, "I have to go. I have to go be with my family. My father-in-law passed away."

On my way home, all I can think of is picking up my daughter and going straight to my son and their dad. All I can picture is our family being together and holding each other in love. You see, up to this point, Michael and I have been in a two-and-a-half-year grueling divorce process after being married for 20 years.

The pivot in our marriage happened a few years ago when I found myself praying to God. I recall sighing deeply before hearing my inner voice say, "I am ready . . . I am ready to see what I have been so afraid to see." I cringed as I heard myself say that, and I was instantly scared about what was going to be revealed to me. The answer came to me a few months later on a Sunday evening.

I am on the way home from a weekend leadership training, and I am so happy to finally be home, take off my work hat, and melt into my family for the rest of the winter. I am hoping to be received with open arms when I arrive. Instead, I am received by a stoic expression and the words, "Oh, you finally decided to come home." My heart drops. I still have my suitcase in my hand. Tonight, I don't even make it past the living room. I end up falling asleep in the living room, curled up into a deflated ball.

The next morning, as I wake up to take the kids to school, he is already gone for work. On my way back from dropping off my kids at their high school, I receive an all too familiar text from Michael that reads, "Are you going to be in the office today, yes or no?" I instantly recognize what the rest of my week is going to be like on the receiving end of his silent treatment. It is in this moment, for the first time in my marriage, I choose to call my older sister to ask her if she is home, and she is.

I stop by our house to get my suitcase that is still in the living room, take the dirty clothes out, and shove a couple of other clean clothes inside. I grab a sweater and head to my sister's house for what I anticipate to be for a day or two, not knowing that this visit will be a point of no return.

Everything goes downhill from here. I painfully see what I have been so petrified to see. I recognize that I am unhappy in my marriage; I feel unsupported and alone. There is nothing that could have prepared me for what is still to come.

I am accused of having an affair. I am accused of loving and choosing my vocation over my family and children. Every time he is able to, he lets me know that I am no longer his family nor ever was a part of the family. One by one, he calls our friends to share our situation with them.

I am entering the darkest season of my soul. I cannot believe how hurtful someone can be whom I have loved so much that I dedicated my life to. He had said I was the love of his life. Before all of this, I had been secretly planning with our two kids to take a trip to Hawaii for our 20th wedding anniversary. The plan was for us to renew our vows with our kids as our witnesses and to have the honeymoon we never had. Painfully, Michael does not believe me.

I am angry, hurt, and feel torn. There is not a day that passes that I am not praying for support, for guidance, for strength, for courage, and for wisdom. I want to do everything in my power to come from love and not affect my family anymore than it is already being affected. I make the decision to file for divorce.

For the next two and a half years, Michael makes every excuse in the book to keep the financials from our corporation from me, which is the last section that needs to be complete in our divorce documents.

Soon after his father's funeral, Michael reaches out to me to share his realization of how their stubbornness got in the way of them reconciling their differences, and how, because of that, he gets to live in regret that his father left this world estranged from his son.

"I know I already lost my wife. Quel, I don't want to lose my best friend too," were Michael's words to me. It is in this moment that our relationship pivots once again, and this time, it's back in the direction of love. We begin to work together to amicably complete our divorce.

In the fourteen months to follow, we have many open-heart conversations. We are generous listeners for each other, recognizing that we were two individuals deeply in love with each other and willing to go to the moon and back to have the other be happy.

By far, my number one passion has always been my family. The loves of my life were my husband, my son and my daughter, and everything I did was for them. I know, without a shadow of a doubt, that if I had known how to, I would have saved my marriage.

Unfortunately, our love for each other was not enough to have our marriage be sustainable. I am now aware that I did not know how to communicate in a way that I could be seen or heard. I recognize that I did not know how to embrace his love nor embrace him with mine. I know now that it was his job to be happy and not mine to make him happy.

A few years later, I send a text to Michael, "Happy Anniversary of the date when we said yes to becoming a family." Amidst all this, Michael has moved on and has two beautiful children.

Whereas I, after this long and intensive dark night of the soul, am ready to embrace love again. In spite of having evidence of the many possible heartbreaks I may be exposed to, I am ready and committed to consciously attract the love of my life and do all of the spiritual work so that my partner and I may grow together in love.

Life's Sweet Song

Janet Langmeier
COLORADO, USA

I am getting ready to go to work when the phone rings. I hear my sister's frantic voice tell me that our brother has suffered a heart attack and has been airlifted to the hospital this morning. In shock and disbelief, I arrange the earliest flight available, throw a few things in a suitcase, and head to the airport.

My brother is four years younger than me. Slim, trim, healthy, strong . . . how is this possible? How can he have three heart blockages? He eats right, and he is physically active—all the things I am not!

For the past two years, I have been dragging myself to work while feeling sick, then coming home from a long day to fall into bed to sleep; and I do it all over again the next day. My life has become a routine of doctors' offices, antibiotics, painkillers, hospitalizations, and emergency rooms. I am sick. I am inactive. I am overweight. If my healthy and active brother can fall like this, what's in store for me?

As I arrive at my brother's bedside later in the day, all of my siblings and their spouses are already at the hospital. I find myself looking around the room at my brothers and sisters, noting how fit and trim each of them is. I keep thinking about how I am the oldest of this bunch and the least healthy. It could easily be me in intensive care!

Over the course of the next few days, our brother is stabilized and released from the hospital. I fly home, reflecting on the abysmal quality of my life. My social life is non-existent because of the state of my health. I am usually not feeling well enough to spend time with family and friends. The activities I once took for granted, such as a simple walk with my dog or going to a movie, are things I no longer have enough energy to do. My life has turned into work, eat, sleep, rinse, and repeat.

The night after I get home, I am sitting in my living room, and I loudly say, "This will not do! I am no longer going to live this way! I need to DO SOMETHING! SOMETHING DIFFERENT! SOMETHING NOW!"

Motivated, I start making a list of things I would love to do. I could try dancing! But in my physical condition, dancing feels like too big of a leap. Hmmm, what else? Traveling would be fun, but getting sick during a trip is too much of a risk. What about singing? This is something I love and might actually be able to do. With this idea in mind, I Google "singing," and Sweet Adeline's International pops up. There are groups meeting nearby in Denver, and a rehearsal is scheduled for Tuesday at a location I know. So, that's that. I decide to go.

Walking into the rehearsal hall on Tuesday night in 2009 is perhaps one of the first times in my life I am making a decision to do something purely for myself. I am not walking in here as a mother, a wife, a sister, a daughter, or a friend. And being unaccustomed to doing things just for me, I feel a strong urge to turn around and run!

A delightful tiny woman with a joyful welcoming smile approaches me. I believe my mouth might be hanging open because as I look around, I see 150 women milling about the floor and the risers! "Janet," this lovely woman, greets me, bringing my attention back to her.

My mind is whirling and spinning on how to escape. "This is our director, Vickie." Although I am feeling trapped, courtesy and politeness take over. I follow Vickie's instructions to follow her. An arpeggio and a Happy Birthday later, I am back with the tiny welcoming woman. She hands me a folder of music and ushers me to the risers, where rehearsal is soon to begin.

With all 150 women now standing on the risers, the woman who welcomed me introduces the guests to the chorus, and Vickie leads the chorus in saying "Hello" as a group to each visitor. I feel a swell in my heart, a lump in my throat, and a thrill that encompasses my entire body as the power and energy of these women's voices flood all of my senses as they say, "Hello!"

Driving home from my first rehearsal, I find myself repeatedly saying, "Wow!" I relive every song and the many warm, inviting hugs from chorus members who encourage me to "come back," telling me that this will "change my life."

This one decision. The decision I make just for me. This decision is changing my life. I keep coming back and learning to sing a cappella four-part harmony. Little do I know that the chorus I join is ranked in the top five choruses in the world! As we prepare for the Regional Competition in the spring of 2010, my health crisis comes to a head. I miss my first Regional Competition as I undergo surgery for the debilitating health issues I have suffered for years.

Although I have only been a member of the chorus for a few months, chorus sisters send me well wishes, visit me at the hospital, and Vickie, our director, calls me to assure me that I will be joining them at the International Competition in Seattle this fall.

As my health improves, I am able to involve myself more deeply in singing. I take voice lessons and revel in learning new music—improving my voice and my ear. The dancing and traveling on my list come to fruition through my chorus experience. Seattle for the International Competition is one of many trips I take with my chorus sisters, and it is so much fun! We work hard at rehearsals preparing for our performance. We also enjoy finding time to take in the sights of Seattle. And the following year, I even land a part in our summer show where I dance on stage in a featured number!

Singing and performing, traveling, and enjoying amazing friendships that all come from that one decision! That one decision is giving me courage and confidence to listen to my voice in other areas of my life, like saying yes to my coaching and teaching career by building my own business. Saying yes to take my children and grandchildren on trips all over the world.

That one decision has opened my heart and opened my life! I am reclaiming my health. I am redefining my work life. I am reaffirming my connections with my family and friends, and I am living a full, rich life that I love! And, of course, I am rediscovering the joy of singing! I am living the pinnacle of life's sweet song.

Generational Healing

Judy Matejczyk
TEXAS, USA

In Akron, Ohio, I am sitting in my rental car, frozen with fear. I look through the windshield and gaze at the building ahead. The sign reads *Assisted Living Center*. My mother is here, and I have not seen her in three years. My teaching job in Texas has kept me busy. I have been too busy with my own kids and grandkids. And I also admit that I have been afraid to see her, as she is old with dementia.

A week ago, I received a phone call from my brother inviting me to come up here and celebrate her 95th birthday. I gave all of the old excuses until he said, "This might be your last chance." And this is what brought me here. I take a deep breath, wipe away my tears, start rehearsing the vision I hold of how the celebration will go, step out of the car, and in I go.

Making my way down the hall, I see my mom sitting in the dining room. As I enter the room, I become surrounded by old people, the smell of old coffee and tuna casserole. She turns her face as I get closer, and our eyes meet. Her eyes are glazed over, and I realize she does not recognize who I am. I smile and say, "Hi, Mom."

At that same moment, my brother heads over to the coffee maker, where he pulls out a coffee filter and places it on top of her head. He bursts out singing Happy Birthday! Everyone almost instantly joins in, and the whole place breaks out in song. My mom bursts into laughter, and the party officially begins.

Next, we take her to my brother's house, and we have the best celebration. At the end of the night, we enjoy the ride while taking her back to the assisted living center. We end the night by giving her a shower and putting her to bed.

As we bathe my 95-year-old mom, I suddenly realize that she bathed us every night as babies, and there were five of us. She would do that for us at the end of a long day, after preparing supper and after the many duties of motherhood. Touching her frail skin and bones is transformational. I can feel immense gratitude.

I sense the spiritual connection in bathing and washing away the past and moving into the new. When that new flesh is frail and fragile at birth and at near death, there is only one bond. I realize, more than ever, the importance of my family back home and how I will soon be the "elder." All the mementos in the house she has been saving, and that I am saving in Texas, mean more than trinkets gathering dust. They become pivotal links to the memories of when our souls met and connected.

The timeline of my own life has a new mark; a new chapter is being written. The release of my physical mother means a new bond with our souls. A whole new wave of gratitude continues. Our family is together one more time, all five of us tonight. There are moments of laughter, tears, and generational releasing as we turn to our family memories before she leaves us physically. And the gratitude I feel from taking the time to celebrate the woman where we all began is so important as we bond before her final journey.

My mother passes one month later. And I am able to look back and know that I completed something important by walking through my fears.

Stepping into My Truth

Beatriz Morales Gil de la Torre

MEXICO

I live in hiding, thinking that if I show who I really am, someone will be upset. These feelings come from living in a home where it bothers people if I speak up and say what I really think, or even laugh out loud. To avoid the anger, I tiptoe around people in every single way. I assume that I must be responsible for how they feel.

Hiding from the world on the outside, I live in a rich and deep inner world, where life is different. This magical place is where I create fun and happy things for me to be absorbed within. In this place, I get to tell myself stories of how I wish things were. I get to imagine people are different for the better. I am hidden. I am safe.

Despite my best efforts to imagine a perfect world, I still never feel good enough. I wonder if I am broken. What if I could better understand what people are thinking? Or what if I could feel their mood changing so I could avoid a stressful situation? In order to walk on my tiptoes, I developed these two skills even more: hide and perceive.

Time goes by, and twenty years have passed now since my marriage. I find myself adapting and doing things to feel loved. I see myself bringing my childhood habits of "hide and perceive" into my marriage. And I still can't seem to let my guard down. Instead of shining bright and stepping into my own shoes in adulthood, I find myself making my presence subdued so other people can be noticed and admired.

I have built my life around making other people comfortable and happy. Why do I do this? It's because I believe that in order to be loved, I have to give up who I am. I don't believe that someone can love me for the simple fact that I am alive. Love always comes with a price. And that price is me.

However, there has always been something inside of me that tells me that there is more than living as someone's shadow. Deep in my heart, I know there is more to life. There has to be a possibility of being myself without having to hide. How do I let go of the fear of making other people upset? How do other people let go? I am unhappy, and I have lived way too long worrying about what everybody thinks!

My family has been falling apart for years, and it's finally happening. It feels like I've lost everything. One of my friends is encouraging me with hope and inspiration. She shares with me, "Now you can do whatever you want!" And as I hear her say these words, I feel paralyzed. I have no idea what I want. And I wonder how I can even begin to imagine a new life I have never experienced? What would that be like?

Despite my best efforts, I am afraid to go to sleep, and I feel lazy to get out of bed. Until one day, I realize enough is enough! I've had it! This cannot be all there is to life! It must be possible to be happy and to feel at peace. There have to be people somewhere in the world who care about other people, who understand that listening is important, who will value what I think and what I feel, who are willing to contribute to the world by being true to themselves—without hiding. I'm tired of hiding, of not being me, and I am tired of not giving myself permission to enjoy who I am. There has to be something that helps me be happy for who I am!

I have always been a deeply spiritual person, and I am convinced that, somehow, we have the power to create whatever we want. I mean, I have already done it a few times throughout my life. It was just doing what had to be done. But this time, I don't know what else to do to be okay. So, I make a plea and ask with all of my might to find a way.

Not too long after I cry out for help, I receive an email inviting me to a class from a mentor I admire. And I accept the invitation! After attending his class, he gives me tickets to a special transformational conference. Even though I'm not clear on the details, something deep within me says I have to be there.

While at the conference, I hear the speaker say, "There is a power in you greater than you think. You are a luminous being living a human experience. When it comes to a life you love living, what would you love?" These words resonate within me. I can feel my spirit suddenly expand beyond the limits of the universe. A part of me awakens as if I have been asleep my entire life until now! I can't stop listening to every word. I am totally absorbed. I feel alive!

As I finish taking notes and start to socialize, I feel absolutely enthusiastic talking with people from all over the world and sharing with them about what I would love in my life! Other people are sharing about how they believe it is important for us all to help one another. The more people I talk to saying the same thing, I think, "Wow! These people have the same heart as I do."

I feel relieved to realize that there are other people in the world who are interested in other people's well-being. And I come to realize an important truth—I am not damaged. I am not broken. I am not alone. I can be me! I want to show myself to the world and for people to learn the beautiful truths I have discovered so that they can enjoy it in their own lives as well. And most importantly, no more hiding.

The Angelic Nurse Who Changes My Life

Susan Wynne Lunning
IOWA, USA

It's early November 1979, and I am sixteen years old. I have a job, neat friends, a boyfriend, and I am diagnosed as pregnant. I'm planning a wedding for November to marry my twenty-year-old boyfriend. I have quite the "attitude," despite the curveball, that I am going to be just fine and that I don't need help from anyone.

One Sunday afternoon after church, I start to feel lower abdominal pain and begin vomiting green material. I expect it to go away, but it continues to happen often. My mother, who, of course, is not pleased with the outcome of her pregnant daughter, is not very understanding.

Mom states, "Don't make such a big deal about it. If you think this is bad, just wait." I proceed to get worse with more and more pain. My mom takes me to my doctor in Minnesota, and he decides to admit me to the hospital but unsupportively states, "Stop hyperventilating. It can't be that bad."

Basically, no one has compassion or sympathy for a pregnant

sixteen-year-old. I feel so low. The treatment theory continues, and as I am admitted to the obstetrics floor, the admitting nurse states very judgmentally as she frowns, "Oh, so now you're pregnant."

After they get me situated, they painfully make sixteen attempts to start an IV before they call the paramedics. There are no apologies or explanations for the trauma I am experiencing. To say I feel overwhelmed is an understatement.

For the next five days, every four hours, they give me a "hypo" shot to "settle me down." I can't eat or drink anything. On Friday night, my doctor walks by my room as I am experiencing another vomiting session. My doctor can see this is not getting any better, so he sets me up with an assessment with a surgeon.

Five minutes into the appointment, he shares, "We are going to do exploratory surgery. I am going to try to save one person instead of losing two." They get to work, and I am being prepared for emergency surgery. I am terrified. My whole body is shaking as I think about what is going to happen. Is everything going to be okay?

As I groggily wake up after the surgery, I ask if the baby is all right. And I am reassured that everything is fine. I have been transferred to the surgery floor after a much-needed salpingo-oophorectomy.

It turns out my ovary and fallopian tube were twisted and full of fluid—much like an appendix ready to rupture. My ovary was found to be the size of a kidney, and my fallopian tube was the size of a banana, full of infectious material ready to be dispersed throughout my entire body. The doctor tells me that I probably would have died later that night without the surgery.

After the surgery, I am weak, and the nurses have to help me with basic needs. The surgery nurses are not talking to me except while they are rolling me over and continuing to make me cough and breathe deep, stating, "Just stop your whining about how much you hurt, and do this." I feel so alone and ashamed.

Then one morning, a small blonde nurse comes in. She stands out as being different. She calls me by my first name, she approaches me with a smile, she respects my choices, and she gives me a bath and a back rub.

During our time together, she picks up on how all I want to do is get better, get married, and raise children. She lovingly visits with me, and she tells me about how important she feels it is to finish school and pursue a career. She says, "It's helpful in case anything happens to your husband, and you would have a way to take care of yourself."

I am starting to feel like she is intruding somewhat on my independence. Until she reluctantly shares that her husband, a deputy sheriff, had been murdered on the job about five months prior. My heart sinks.

She goes on to disclose that if she did not have her education and job, it would have been so much harder for her to adjust. I know I will never forget her, what she is saying, and how it feels to be treated with such compassion during this difficult time of my life. I start to detach from my anger and what I have been going through. I start to feel true healing.

Years later, in 1996, my mother has hysterectomy surgery in the same hospital and on the same floor. I drive 500 miles to be with her. After arriving at the hospital, I ask the nurses if the nurse from my own surgery is still working there, and I share why I am interested in talking with her. The nurses are delighted to contact her for me!

The next afternoon, I hear the phone ring in my mother's room at the hospital. I pick up the phone, and it's my nurse. I explain, "Many years ago, you changed a young girl's heart." And I give her a description of myself and my life today. I go on to tell her how I have three children, I live in Iowa, I am a registered nurse, and I am working on my Bachelor of Science in nursing.

With joy, I share about how every time I work with a patient, I feel a responsibility to earn their trust because of the positive impact that can be made to change a person's life. She starts crying because she is overwhelmed with what I've shared. She is humbled and so grateful to hear how she made a difference because really all she did was listen and care about my outcome in life. But that was everything to me.

A New Chapter

Dana Consuelo
WASHINGTON, USA

It's a chilly winter morning in the Pacific Northwest. Rain has been falling steadily most of the night. As I look out the window of my office, I notice the fog is beginning to lift. I am on my first coaching call of the day as my client begins by telling me, "I am grateful for the tools I have learned in my program because last night's dinner with my dad and brother was actually pleasant!

"Instead of the usual tense experience that would lead to conflict, I was able to be compassionate towards my father and his struggle instead of being pulled into his angry drama about his housing situation. I am so grateful for this dream-building process. I can't imagine dealing with my father and brother without these new tools."

After our call, I gaze again through my window and begin to reflect on how I have come to this happy moment. It all started two years ago. I had recently returned from Virginia to live once again close to my family. I had retired from my successful career in the healing arts and was looking for another purpose in my life. I wanted to continue to serve people and have an income stream too.

Since my return, I had been spending several days a week with my disabled son. I would help him get caught up on medical appointments, clean his apartment, shop for groceries, and prepare meals.

Through his social worker, I discovered there was a federally funded program for assistance with home care, and he qualified. I decided to take the training and officially become his health care aide. In addition to my son, I soon began to help other disabled people as an HCA. In that moment, it seemed like a good direction to follow—to still be of service and have a stream of income.

In hindsight, I have to say, this was the most humbling work I have ever done. I wiped bottoms, I cleaned up filthy bathrooms, and I lifted walkers and wheelchairs in and out of my Ford Fiesta sedan. One morning, I had dropped one of the removable wheels of my disabled client's wheelchair on my big toe, and oh, that hurt!

The job was really starting to catch up with me. Looking back, I can now see this was a soft signal that this was not the best way to use my gifts and talents. But, in that moment, I just told myself to stay calm and soldier on.

One day, I was sitting beside an elderly client on her old saggy couch, watching her favorite cop show, NCIS. The theme of this show was so sinister, and the scenes were so violent that I closed my eyes, slipped my hands over both ears, and began to hum quietly to drown out the noise coming from the TV. I suddenly felt trapped. My initial enthusiasm to be of service as an HCA suddenly evaporated, and I knew I had to make a change. I would do whatever it took.

When I went home that night, I was determined to find

something I could do, but I began to feel uncertain and scared about quitting. I thought, "What if I fail to find something else?" This voice within me was arguing with my decision to make a change, saying, "You're too old to do anything else, and any more changes will be hard to manage." But another part of me knew from past experiences that great opportunities never show up when it's convenient or easy. Great things occur on the other side of comfortable.

So, I made the decision to let the part of me that wanted to be of service, and be happy and fulfilled doing it, win over the part of me that was afraid. I believed there had to be a better way. And I was going to find it.

Several weeks later, I was telling my mentor Donna my predicament. She paused, looked straight at me, and asked, "What do you love doing now?" I sat up a little straighter and said confidently, "I love being a prayer chaplain at my Unity church." She smiled at me and responded, "Why don't you look into becoming a spiritual counselor of some kind?" Then she mentioned how her good friend, who had retired from being a full-time minister, was now working from home as a part-time spiritual counselor and making good money doing so. Immediately, a flash of insight came into my awareness, and I knew this could be an answer to my discontent. Driving home, I felt a twinge of excitement and hope.

That night, I started researching what it would require to be a prayer chaplain beyond the walls of my church. I looked into being a prayer chaplain in hospital settings, and I found that required becoming a minister. When I looked at various traditional counseling or coaching programs, I realized what I really wanted was spiritually based training.

As I was pacing my small apartment, determined to change the trajectory of my life and needing a clue for where to look, I noticed in my bookcase a boxed set of CDs from an inspiring program I had taken five years before that, taught by a former Unity minister. Feeling hopeful, I Googled the minister and up popped her online institute.

As I clicked through the website, I saw that not only did her company have programs for bettering people's understanding of how to live life in harmony with spiritual laws, but she also had training to become a certified spiritual coach of these programs! I was thrilled! This could be the path I'd been seeking! That day I applied. Three days later, after a lengthy interview, I was accepted into the full training program to become a certified life coach.

As I went through the rigorous study, I remember distinctly how I felt a continuous sense of joy knowing this was an answer to my deep longing to do more with my skills and to give more from my unique gifts. In the months that followed, I prioritized my life. I studied every day, and I let go of certain people (yes, the cop show client is now history) and activities that didn't serve my dream. Most importantly, I achieved my goal of becoming a certified life coach!

As I come out of my reflective thoughts, I notice it's time for my weekly group coaching call. After a quick stretch, I dial into the conference call number and greet my clients with a cheerful hello. Each client begins checking in by sharing what they are grateful for today.

The last woman in the group gives me a precious gift of appreciation that confirms to me that I am on the right path. With a deep sigh, she slowly says, "I am so grateful I joined this class. I have learned things about myself that I could not have learned on my own. Your support has made all the difference."

Gift of Healing

Hollie Kikel
COLORADO, USA

As I close my eyes, I have no idea what is about to happen. I tell myself to be open and to receive. The physical and emotional pain is overwhelming, and there is a part of me that doesn't believe I can make it through this.

These thoughts run through my mind as I sit in my living room in Colorado, listening to an energy healer online from California. She is speaking to our soulful group, gathered for the common purpose of healing individually and collectively.

How can this work? This internal voice of doubt echoes in my mind loud and clear. Energy healing isn't new to me, but I've always participated and received it in person, never remotely. I believe remote healing is possible, so I push my skeptic mind aside while I let the pull of curiosity win.

My wrist and hands are swollen. They are unable to move and severely bruised from a surgery that hadn't gone as planned.

Physical therapy is painfully slow, and my surgeon had told me I might not regain the full use of my hand.

For the past few years, I have been ignoring the signs my body was sending. I tell myself that I don't have the time to be down for a few weeks, and I should just grin and bear it. Or I tell myself that it's selfish to focus on myself with all the responsibilities I have.

Stepping back into my memories, I remember caring for my mother in the last stage of her life. These seven years have been my complete focus and purpose. It has also been an excuse to ignore my own life—my health, relationships, and career. My mother's dementia and emphysema are getting worse. Even though my siblings and I have made the difficult decision to get more help and place her in a facility a few years ago, I can still barely keep up with her doctors' appointments, coordinate the care she needs, and spend quality time with her.

What starts out as a duty turns into a beautiful lesson in patience and compassion. Our relationship deepens even as her mind slowly starts slipping away. And, near the end, I promise my mother I will return to focusing on my life and that I will make the changes that have kept prodding me through signs. I realize later that these signs are the Universe guiding me to a new path.

After two long months of hospital stays, rehab, and finally nursing home care, my mother makes her transition surrounded by her loving children. It is a sacred experience that is at the same time heartbreaking and enlightening. Being a witness to her transition, I know my mother's soul did not die. Only her physical body, which no longer serves a beautiful, lively spirit that is ready for her next journey, dies.

This moment prompts me to ask, "Am I ready for a new journey in my life?" I feel lost, scared, uncertain of my future. Suddenly, there is no one else to take care of except me. Now, there are no excuses to ignore my own life. So, I have finally taken my first step, and I got the wrist surgery a few months later. Although it's painful, it gives me a chance to pause my life, grieve, and heal. And it also gives me an unexpected gift.

Brought back into the present moment, I listen to the healer as she begins to slowly take us into the session with her soft voice. Breathing slowly and closing my eyes as I listen, I relax as she goes silent. A few minutes later, I begin to feel waves of energy in my body. It is undeniable, the connection to Source I am feeling. I have experienced this once before with a gifted healer on a retreat in Sedona, Arizona, but I never thought I would be able to experience this remotely.

Midway through the session, something amazing happens. My lifeless hand suddenly has a surge of energy flow through it, and it feels like it is moving in circles. I keep my eyes closed, not allowing my skeptical mind to interfere. I hadn't been expecting anything, so I'm not making this happen. I am simply allowing it to happen, and I'm going with the flow.

After the session, I feel peace, calm, and a oneness with Spirit that I've never felt before. My curiosity is stoked. I receive more healing sessions, and my hand begins to strengthen. The physical therapy starts to reap results more quickly. As if beautifully mirrored to me by my body, I begin to open up to life again—as my once lifeless hand begins to function.

As I make my way back to work, I feel much stronger. A few weeks go by, and the Universe is sending me another sign. I receive an invitation to become a healer and to train with the institute that gave me my healing. I feel drawn to do it, but again the voices of doubt and fear speak up. "Who am I to do something like this? I'm too old to make changes in my life right now!"

When something is meant to be, the desire becomes greater than the fear. I decide to go for it anyway! I start practicing with my fellow healing students and putting in long hours during my evenings and weekends whenever I can fit it in. I don't mind the extra effort because the thought of helping someone heal the way I was gives me a sense of purpose I have never felt before.

My first client session is with my niece, who has never experienced energy healing before but is open to it. My doubts and fears speak up again. These thoughts try to convince me that she's not going to feel anything and that I am going to make a fool of myself. Once again, I let the pull to do this be stronger than the discouraging voices.

At the end of the session, my niece opens her eyes, and she has a look of amazement on her face. She begins telling me about how she felt her body floating with waves of energy flowing through her, and she describes being on a journey to another place in time and space.

In this moment, I realize something important. If I had listened to those voices of doubt and fear, I never would have discovered the healer within me, and I would never have gone forward to help others heal. The voices of doubt and fear still come up as I push myself beyond my comfort zone. But as I have expanded to also learn and grow through my life coaching training, I can clearly see that the voices of doubt and fear are actually not red flags at all. They are good signs that I am growing, expanding, and discovering my truth.

Trusting the Universe

Julie Castle
CALIFORNIA, USA

From the outside looking in, you might think I am living a happy and fulfilling life. I am married, own a successful business with my husband, have three wonderful children, plenty of money, a beautiful home, investment property, tons of friends, and an active social life. I mean, what more can you want? I am living the American Dream, right?

Wrong! My marriage has been on the rocks for years, but we keep up appearances for a multitude of reasons, most of which revolve around our business image. I didn't know how to do it or when I would do it, but I knew I was leaving this marriage. I don't believe the reasons for leaving are important to this story. I'm sure there are plenty of people who might say I gave up, or I didn't fight hard enough, or some other judgment based on whatever explanation I provide. So, I'll simply say, I had to leave the marriage because I was no longer a healthy person in it.

After years and years of trying couples counseling, consulting self-help books, and confiding in friends, I finally decide to contact a divorce attorney to start the process of what I think is either going to save me or end me. Either way, I have come to this point. I decide I have to leave, or I will die.

As I sob in my car, in a parking lot in the middle of the afternoon, I pick up my phone. I search by typing in "divorce attorney," and I call the first one on the list. After a quick 20-minute call and an appointment to meet in person the next day, my life changes almost instantly.

I know one of the first things I need to do next is find a job. I get on the computer, update my resume, and start applying for any and every job I find that sounds remotely interesting. Whether I am qualified or not doesn't matter much at this moment, nor does the pay. I am taking action, and that action is what is moving me in the direction of my dreams, even though I am not fully aware of that yet.

I know I need to find a new place to live, and suddenly, or so it seems, I am noticing how many houses are for rent in the area I would love to live in. I start to make appointments to view them, even though I have no idea what I can afford.

Within four months, I have a new part-time job at the local high school with a schedule that still allows me to easily get the kids to and from school every day. I also agree to sell my half of the company to my husband; however, I continue to work in the photography industry as a mentor and coach for other photographers and photography companies nationwide. My favorite part is guiding them closer to their entrepreneurial goals.

On top of all of this coming together, I move into a cute four-bedroom house that is just big enough for the kids and me. I start over with all new furniture and appliances, which at the time seems to be costing me a fortune, but I am trusting the process and leaving the details alone. It isn't time for me to figure out how I will pay for all of it. It is more important to keep moving forward. I have to believe that the Universe will work with me. It is scary, to say the least, but there is power in doing it anyway. My life is already changing for the better!

One day as I am scrolling through Facebook, I see an ad to become a life coach. I watch it and think it's interesting, but I convince myself that I am too old and don't have the money to invest in starting a new career. I dismiss the ad. But I see this ad the next day and the next day. I continue to dismiss it repeatedly! Until about the fifth or sixth time I see it, I decide that maybe, just maybe, this is a message from the Universe and that I might want to listen better. So, I did.

I go to my first transformational conference hosted by the life coaching company, and I know by the end of the weekend that this is my calling, to become a certified life coach. I invest in myself that weekend and take control over who I am and what I want to contribute to this world. Starting a new career on the heels of a divorce, financial strain, being a single mom to three teenagers, and struggling with bouts of depression and anxiety are challenges I had never known before.

I still get stuck on myself sometimes, but having the coaching and training that I have received as a life coach is what gives me the strength to persevere, strive, and thrive through it all. The Universe listens to what we say and shows up for us all the time, but it's our job to recognize it and act on it.

Unexpected Companion

Susan Kennedy

TEXAS, USA

Since moving from my roots in Virginia to Texas some 30 odd years ago, I have been enjoying the heart-warming experience of annually visiting my family and friends. Every time, without fail, I have an excited anticipation of "going home" as I pack, drive to the airport, and receive greetings from my family waiting for me at the airport.

It's December as I head to the airport. This is no exception. I am filled with excitement! But I also know this trip to Virginia is different, and I sense it is also going to be that way from this point forward. Mom is no longer living in her own home. My family will not be waiting for me at the airport. Yet, I still have that feeling of "coming home."

This trip is to celebrate my mom's 88th birthday. My sisters and I are planning a surprise birthday party for her in the Memory Care Unit where she lives. I shipped a special birthday gift to her to arrive when I get there. We also invited all of her favorite people, including her brother, all of us grown kids, grandkids, and great-grandkids, and a few special friends. Dana, her favorite caregiver, is in on the surprise, and she is helping set up the party.

When it comes to her presents, my mom is not easy to choose gifts for. I am continually laboring over—do I get her a box of her favorite candy, Turtles? Maybe some new socks or a blanket? Nothing is feeling quite right for my mom's gift. As I search for her present online, I find an article about people diagnosed with dementia and how they love stuffed animals and dolls. Mom loves dogs, but really? A toy dog? I am afraid she will be insulted.

As I scroll, I find a fluffy yellow toy dog with an adorable face that even I can't resist. It moves and whimpers like a little puppy. The description reads, "Increases feelings for comfort and security," "Encourages nurturing feelings," and "Reduces symptoms like agitation, depression, and feelings of isolation." PERFECT! This sounds like exactly what she needs. She hasn't been enjoying being "locked up" with "those people."

During my mom's younger years, she had been a super-smart, fiercely independent woman, living alone in her own home until nine months prior. She hates being in the Memory Care Unit. As a matter of fact, she resists any type of limitations being placed on her.

Although she can no longer get around without a walker or a wheelchair and assistance, she still believes she can. Often our talks center around what she is going to do when she gets out of there. I listen with love as she continues to live her life in her mind while we have these conversations. She lives with a lot of frustration and anger, as her disease isn't allowing her to process everything happening to her.

A lot of experts note that a surprise and lots of people will only agitate someone with dementia. Even with her dementia, we decide to keep this day and party for her, knowing she will benefit from feeling love, and she also loves attention. I know my mom.

It's morning, and I head over to the Memory Care Unit to visit her before the big birthday party. The celebration is later tonight, but I can't wait to give her the present. I hand her the puppy. My heart melts, and I am filled with pure joy as I see my mom's face light up, beaming with happiness. The toy dog whimpers and moves as it's turned on. She immediately starts hugging and talking to her new puppy. You can feel her love and warmth for her new friend.

An hour later, she asks me if her new puppy needs to eat. Thinking she is joking and then realizing she is serious, I explain, "He can only have water from your finger to his lips." She also asks, "Does he need to go outside for the bathroom?" She is in love. Now she has a companion, someone to love, and a purpose.

As I roll her into the cafeteria for lunch, she proudly carries her puppy in her lap, getting lots of positive attention from the other residents. It would end up being the talk of the lunch table for months to come. After lunch, my mom settles into her bed for a nap. I give her time to rest while I head over to pick up two ice cream cakes for the celebration. Friends and family start to arrive, and once I get everything set up in the cafeteria, I go to get my mom.

She is sound asleep on her sofa with a smile on her face and that sweet puppy snuggled between her arms. I stand and breathe in this peaceful moment. She hasn't experienced this much peace since coming to live here.

As she begins to wake up, she talks to the puppy and gives him sweet good morning kisses. I let her know that Dana, her favorite person in the world, wants to see her in the living area. After a few minutes of getting ready, she gets in the wheelchair and off we go, with her sweet puppy, of course.

As we round the corner to the cafeteria, she immediately lights up when she sees Dana. She has to show him her new puppy. It takes her a minute, and then she suddenly recognizes her brother. She starts to discover more and more of her family and friends. It was after this moment that she realizes that this is a gathering for her. She forgot it's her birthday, but we are not going to let her feel forgotten.

With Dana sitting beside her, she beams with joy as she talks with everyone. We have cake, take pictures, and we eventually say our good-byes to family and friends. It was a wonderful day. There is so much love to go around. My mom's spirit has been lifted during this special day. My spirit has been lifted for a lifetime.

Cup of Serenity

Valerie Whetstone
CALIFORNIA, USA

I open my eyes to the sound of a nuclear attack. It takes a few seconds for my brain to realize it is just my alarm clock. The time is flashing 6:35 a.m. Are you kidding me? Already? I just closed my eyes! I bolt from my bed into my closet to put on my clothes. I take a quick peek in the bathroom mirror to fluff my hair, brush my teeth, and begin every day just like the last one.

I go downstairs, feed the dog and let him outside, start making chocolate chip pancakes for my kids, stuff all of their homework from last night into their backpacks, make lunches for the entire family, fill up water bottles, help get my kids dressed, brush their hair, try to coerce them to brush their teeth, grab their jackets as they complain about having to carry it all day, grab the car keys, jump in my blue minivan, and head to the parent drop zone at school.

While in the line for drop-off, I rehearse spelling words with my youngest child for his test today. "R U N spells run. S T O P spells stop." All while quizzing my oldest on his multiplication facts. As I glance down and take a look at my pants, my eyes widen in disbelief. Holy Cow!

Staring at me are cute little Hello Kitty faces on my pajama bottoms. As cute as they are, I realize I forgot to put on my pants!!! All I can think is *Please, don't make me get out of this car.* I tell my kids, "Make sure you are ready to hop out of the car! I love you, and have a wonderful day!"

As I pull into the driveway of my house, I contemplate what in my life has to change. But what is it? How do I figure it out? There has got to be more to life. I am literally the energizer bunny all the time, and I am so tired. So, I rewarm my tea from earlier this morning and decide to sit on the couch before running my errands. Something I never do!

As I sit motionless, I take a few breaths and look around my family room. I notice the warmth of the mug I am holding, and I see the word "peace" in gold lettering on the cup. I smell the fresh aroma of chamomile and lavender from my tea.

My whole body starts to feel open, relaxed, and free. I stare at the mug as if it is magical. I start to wonder what is happening. It is as if someone is whispering to me, *Relax.* I look around the room again and notice how quiet it is. Everything is perfectly still! I glance at the family portrait over the fireplace, and a smile forms in my heart. I am truly glowing from the inside out.

Goodness, my kids, how sweet and innocent they look. Wow, my husband has a full head of hair! I place my hands across my heart. I begin breathing in and out. We all look so happy. I actually feel the warmth of the memories this picture captures. I think to myself, *Wow, my kids have sure grown up. Where has the time gone?* The phrase "stop and smell the roses" comes to mind.

Oh my gosh, I get it. The phrase isn't just talking about nature, but to actually slow down and be present! My mouth drops, and I begin to let it all sink in. How beautiful this feels. I say out loud to myself, "Gosh, I need to take a moment each day in my life to actually unwrap the gift of the present. Could it be, I discovered the secret of true bliss, and it is as simple as this?"

Later in the evening my husband asks me, "How was your day?" as he always does. However, my response is a little different. "It was beautiful! Today, I realized that the sweetest things in life are free. There's a whole lot more to life than pushing around all in worry." He smiles at me. I ask him if he would like to share a cup of tea with me. He responds, "Sure!" So, I grab the tea box from earlier and see a little message on the tea bag tag. It says, "Serenity."

Pull Up the Anchor

Julie Carlisle
UTAH, USA

One night, fate knocks on my door, or in a modern fashion, texts me. My neighbor's sister, Nikki, is in town, and she is offering foot zone sessions. Her sister is said to have a special gift of picking up on certain things about people, which intrigues me. My husband is out of town, and I am free. So I think why not?

At the home next door, Nikki gives me a wonderful foot zone, and she comments about how she is able to sense that I am a deeply spiritual person. As she nears the end of the foot zone session, she inhales and says, "You have the biggest heart I have ever felt."

While saying this, she is zoning the ball of my left foot, and I think, "Okay, that's interesting."

"Have you ever thought about doing this work?" she asks in reference to foot zoning.

"Yes," I reply, "quite often, and my husband is often encouraging me to learn more about it."

She seems surprised! She asks, "Then why are you not trained?"

149

I would love to learn foot zoning, but I haven't taken it seriously. I figure I will learn someday, when the time is right, and all of my obstacles are gone.

The next day, as I am showering, I hear a voice, as if it were next to me, say, "It's time for you to do it!" This voice is soft, peaceful, familiar, and I know it isn't my own. Deep down, I also know exactly what it's referring to. My immediate response is that there's no way because I don't have the money. The voice replies, "Yes, you do. It's time to do it."

Suddenly, I remember the tax return we just received, and I also realize it happens to be the exact amount I will need! I can feel confidence wash over me, that all of the possible obstacles will be removed, and I am going to learn how to foot zone. As I think about this opportunity, I start to understand and believe that this is destined for my life. Everything is lining up.

After my shower, I start looking into training, and there is even a new class starting next week! I jump in with everything I have, and I learn how to foot zone. It is truly miraculous how everything is coming together after making my decision. Time goes on, and I am absolutely in love with healing others through this amazing modality. I continue to learn other healing methods as well.

Not too long after pursuing my new practice, a friend calls me and offers a free ticket to an energy conference. I have never been to one before, but I happily accept the ticket. The conference is two hours away, but on that day, I happen to be going that direction for another appointment just down the road. I see this as an amazing coincidence and opportunity.

I love the energy conference and learn many valuable things from amazing practitioners. There is one more presentation I want to attend but know I will have to leave early for my appointment. It is a woman speaking on prosperity and mindset. Never before have I heard anything remotely close to what this woman is teaching, and it blows my mind! Money is energy?! What?! I am so intrigued with what she is saying that I have to peel myself out of my chair to make it to my appointment in time.

Needless to say, I look this lady up, and I sign up for group coaching with her. The course she offers is based on prosperity, but I find all areas of my life-transforming as I do the work. My whole attitude changes, and I lose 20 lbs. in four months without even trying! I had tried everything to lose that weight for the last 20 years! I manifest my goal of making a specific amount of money every month, and I continue to manifest that money goal consistently every month! This is the most amazing and fun thing I have done in a long time.

I can feel the old vibrant me returning as I turn limiting beliefs that have been running the show into positive thoughts and vibrations. I begin to feel a deep desire to teach these principles to others, along with the healing modalities I practice.

Fate knocks on my door once again, bringing me another amazing mentor! Not only does this woman teach me about transformation and life mastery, but she also has a school where I can train and certify to begin coaching. It all happens so fast, and I find myself on a phone call to become a student at her coaching institute. The call is empowering. I feel truly inspired! I know this is what I am meant to do next! I have always offered others advice and healing, so why not start a new business doing what I absolutely love anyway?

So, on this warm autumn day in October, I sign up to become a certified coach. And I am sorry to say it isn't only peaceful new beginnings! I totally freak out after the phone call. What have I just done? I just invested a whole lot of money and time into what? Me? Coaching? I am happy with my corporate job and foot zone sessions. Who do I think I am to coach other people like the powerful mentors I have seen? What should I do now? I take a deep breath, and I go for a walk.

As I walk around the block, calming my thoughts, a vision comes across my mind. A vision of a boat docked in a beautiful bay. The image is soothing to me, and in this moment, a voice asks, "Do you like being a ship docked in the bay?"

"Why yes," I answer. "It's safe and calm here inside the bay."

And then my mind opens up, and I am sailing! I mean, I could really feel the wind in my hair and the smell of the sea! This feeling is so exhilarating and free. "Oh!" I agree, "I want to sail!" I can't help but say it again a bit louder. "I want to sail!!" As I come back to awareness in the present moment, I realize I am standing there on the sidewalk and that I may have said everything out loud.

I ponder this experience in my mind and realize that the boat in the bay is safe but also stuck. The sailboat is free, and it has so many options. This is what I am doing by allowing myself to stay where I am because it is safe. I am suffering with discontent and longing by staying in my corporate job and choosing not to do what I am meant to be doing.

I realize in this moment that if I stay stuck where I am, it may be safe, but ultimately it will cause me pain. I want to learn new things, help others in meaningful ways, and grow. I am given this beautiful vision to show me that I must pull up the anchor that has kept me stuck in the bay and begin to sail. "I really do want to sail!"

It's Never Too Late

Nancy McCulloch

TEXAS, USA

It's November of 2006, and I find myself in my mid-fifties, out of work, deep in debt, and feeling completely stuck. I admire people who work steadily all of their lives and are able to retire comfortably. A part of me wants that. But here I am, 55 years old, and the average retirement age is only ten years away. I am nowhere near my dream of a comfortable retirement.

All of my adult life, I have read and studied human potential and development. It started when I read Maxwell Maltz's book *Psycho-Cybernetics* in the early 1970s. Deep down, even as a young child, I have always known that there is a power within everyone that can be tapped to create miracles if we just know how to understand it and work with it. I have the knowledge, but it seems I have never felt compelled to implement it until now.

As I think about these things, something wells up inside of me, and I can feel a strong determination that, somehow, I am not going to allow a dire future of being too old to work, unwanted in the workforce, and no financial security to be my fate. I make a decision to finally implement this knowledge of success. The success that I have denied myself my entire life.

It starts with acknowledging the power that is within me, that is within all of us, the power that is everywhere, a power that is loving, and a power that wants the best for its creation. I call this power God. Others may call it by another name. As I call upon this power, I feel reassurance that I am deserving of a bright future.

I clearly visualize myself as already having a steady job in a strong, secure place of employment, with opportunities for growth, and retirement benefits. I feel the joy, gratitude, and grounding feelings that I already have it. I envision myself as retired with a substantial income and retirement savings. It feels so real! I can feel the peace and joy within. I convince myself that I already have it, and it is mine to keep.

The next thing I do is decide to take action for this new chapter of life. I start applying for jobs at the types of places I previously thought I would never be considered. One of the places I am applying to is a state-sponsored major medical university.

As I apply, I have no clue about the details or the benefits. I mainly see it as a place that offers security and promotion opportunities. Even while stepping forward in my newly discovered determination, I cannot in my wildest dreams think I will ever be contacted by them since thousands of people apply there each month.

Much to my amazement, the HR department of this institution contacts me the day after I apply! They ask me, "Can you come in tomorrow for an interview?" And I was like, of course! I arrive at the interview early, check in with the receptionist, and wait about ten minutes.

After this short wait, I am told, "The HR manager who set up your appointment and interview is out of the office due to a death in her family. She will contact you when she returns to work and reschedules your appointment." I am sympathetic towards the manager, but at the same time, I feel confused and disappointed.

I head out of the building, get back to my car, and start driving home. I've driven about 15 minutes, and as I think about everything that just happened, I receive a phone call from the HR manager's office. They tell me that she decided to come into the office so she can interview me. I am shocked. Why would she leave her family and friends during the trauma she is experiencing just to interview me? Nevertheless, I turn the car around and head back for the interview.

After my initial interview, the HR manager assigns me to ten interviews over the next two weeks. Almost all of them offer me a position. I am so surprised and so honored! After exploring my options, I select a position—and it's a position with a salary much higher than I have ever made in my life! This institution also grants me a pension, excellent medical benefits, and a retirement savings plan, and there are more opportunities for promotions than I have ever encountered before.

About six months after starting my job, I am on the phone with the HR manager who helped me get the position. I share, "I appreciate you coming in to interview me while you were dealing with a death in your family. I hope your family is healing from the loss." She then makes a statement that I will never forget. "There was a certain something about you and your qualifications that stood out to me. I knew that we needed to hire you and not let you get away." To this day, I have no idea what she saw in me, but I know that I owe it to the higher power that is available to us all.

Over the years I have been working here, I am rising through the ranks. My debt is now paid off, I have savings for retirement, and I am able to retire with a comfortable income and retirement savings. I am amazed at how it all worked out. The success principles I have studied and read for most of my life are proving to be true. All it took was the determination to put them into practice.

Love Made Visible

Marilyn K. Lawrence
CALIFORNIA, USA

Trading years of wanderlust and experiencing varied work experiences, my prince charming and I return to the west coast, as the film industry says, with a giant adventure in the can. A forever California girl, I am near ecstatic as I unpack my work-life stories while feeling the warmth of the sunshine. Life is unfolding in a way that brings me joy. Or so I think.

Thirteen months later, I am no longer ecstatic, and instead, hit by shock. It's shock from the inconsolable loss of my prince, who dies suddenly after an unexpected surgery. The doctors say that Larry's heart is bad, but I know they are wrong. I know he has a sweet heart, and my heart's the one that's breaking. Wistful for the fleeting, precious time leading up to surgery, I cherish a favor he asks of his nurse, "Please tilt the angle of the bed so I can see my wife."

In that morning gloom, after the practitioner turns off the heart rate monitor, a hospital chaplain offers spiritual care to my daughter Jill and me. We are grateful for the chaplain as he brings coherence to our anguish and despair, offering the suggestion to "Honor Larry's memory by following his good example." Naturally, Jill and I act on this encouragement as Larry's unique influence is richly imprinted on our minds.

Once time dulls the rawness of my grief and feeling stuck, I return to writing work-life essays for my daybook *Office Confidential*. Around then, during a silent meditation, a relevant epiphany emerges, conveying the essence of Larry as being the epitome of what Sigmund Freud expresses as, "Love and work . . . work and love, that's all there is." Accordingly, Kahlil Gibran echoes, "Work is love made visible."

These attributes truly fit Larry as he had genuinely infused love into everything. In fact, his final social media banner had read, "Love One Another." Besides, no gesture was too trivial for him, including picking raisins out of Raisin Bran to make my favorite hot cereal or fabricating a copper third hand for Jill's shampoo.

Admiring friends eulogize that "Larry made the best chocolate chip cookies and cheesecake on the planet and sang Bob Dylan better than Bob Dylan." Moreover, my prince consistently made love visible in the beauty of his art, be it lost-wax jewelry, inlay designs, ornamental ironworks, furniture restorations, musical instruments, or sculptures.

Ironically, while Larry forged all that is golden from our own backyard, I chased an eclectic and ideal work-life coast to coast in my quest to gather compelling essay material. A one-of-a-kind husband, Larry also assumed a majordomo role, spoiling me daily. His devotion was cheerful and given with flair. Serving morning coffee and evening meals, for instance, was always played up with a twirl and a bow. I will forever love his way of being human.

Fast-forward three years, and I am considering a dramatic change when an email from my first spiritual teacher invigorates what I affectionately refer to as my lifelong journey—the journey inward. Researching his recommendation of a premier institute for transformation, I discover an intriguing curriculum focused on the science of creating dreams, and it perfectly complements my professional and personal goals.

I decide here and now to become a certified life coach as it is clear that I not only want this course of study, but I also need its rigorous structure and accountability. I need its systematic process of transformation.

Further up the road, I understand the ultimate gift of my "Gulliver's Travels." Going over the peaks and valleys, and even during my coaching pathway, I realize it's not about auspicious accomplishments. The ultimate gift of this journey is my deeper connection to the inner world and sense of oneness with the universe. I realize there is only an illusion of separation. Because only one life is breathing through and as me, through and as my prince, and through and as everyone else.

The beauty is knowing that through all of this, there is a beautiful purpose. All of this is how love is made visible.

Encountering Little Spiderman

Rebecca J Wright

CALIFORNIA, USA

I see that look on her face, the expression of a mother beyond exhaustion. Two of the boys are standing in the checkout line close to their father. However, the smallest child dressed in Spiderman pajamas and with bare feet on the concrete floor is the one that really catches my attention. He stands just behind his siblings and father, holding on to his miniature "shopping in training" cart with its high rising flag.

The young boy looks up at me as I step into the checkout line behind him, and I smile back. His Spiderman pajamas are striking—complete with padded muscles, and it's probably his favorite clothing item. There is no doubt that he is a child full of energy during all of his waking hours.

Suddenly, the mother runs back to grab a grocery item she must have forgotten. Just as she leaves, the cashier asks the little Spiderman boy to hand her the only item in his miniature shopping cart—a box of cookies. He is reluctant to part with his prized merchandise. Every time the cashier reaches for the cookies, he loudly protests with his three-year-old insistence.

Since his father is not offering a solution, I lean down and encourage him, "Watch, and you will see how the cashier puts your box of cookies at the other end of the counter after she checks it. It's so, after that, you get to take it home." He sizes me up, considering my suggestion with large eyes and hesitation, then gives up the cookies to the cashier.

Unfortunately, the cashier is not paying attention to me or what I shared. Instead of moving the cookies to the other side, she continues to hold on to the box while she chats with the boys' father. The little Spiderman boy takes his miniature shopping cart behind his father and brothers to the other end of the counter to retrieve his cookies. He is just tall enough to see over the top edge of the checkout stand when he stands on tiptoe, but there are no cookies!

He again starts vocalizing his frustrations, and this time, even louder. His five-year-old brother joins in with needs of his own, and at this point, I cannot get the cashier's attention to put the cookies back into the little Spiderman's shopping cart so all can be well.

Suddenly, I see little Spiderman grab his miniature cart and take off running toward the store's front automatic sliding door! I watch the little attached flag gaining speed as he nears the exit to the parking area. I feel anxiety, but I'm not sure what to do! Miraculously, his mother appears, as if by magic, to intercept her youngest son just in time before he can escape. The whole family reunites at the checkout stand to finish their purchase.

By now, the cashier and both parents just want to finish the transaction and make it out of the store with their family intact. The receipt is finally handed to the father while the children's mayhem continues. The father asks the cashier, "Do you have any suckers?" She quickly pulls a basket out from under the counter. Everyone's eyes are glued to the basket. EMPTY!

Little Spiderman starts a high-pitched whine that increases in loudness and intensity while our cashier frantically asks the other cashiers if anyone has suckers at their neighboring stations. Alas, not one sucker is at any of their stations!

I purposely chose the shortest checkout line in the store behind this family because I am on a very short lunch break from work. The escalation now unfolding is not in my plan to get back to work with my quick salad purchase and into my corporate cubicle on time. Of course, scheduled timeliness has its merits. Yet, I believe how one reacts and responds in a seemingly random slot of time is just as important. The situation definitely will not be helped by impatient words and action. I take a moment to decide to center inward, consciously breathe slowly, and think, "Just be here and now."

Perhaps it is experience in raising a son or just being open to my intuition, but an idea pops into my head in the midst of the chaos. Behind me, there is one empty checkout stand. Instantly, I step into the forbidden sacred space by the cash register, and I find the key to the situation at hand—a full basket of suckers. I pull out the immediate sweet solution to the now escalated problem.

With a quick silent prayer of gratitude to the Universe, I hand the basket to the frantic and surprised cashier. The little boys instantly become quiet while picking out their favorite flavor. All is right with the world!

While finally driving back to work with my salad, I ponder the drama of this brief yet eventful experience. Perhaps my placement into this particular time and place is not a random event. For me, this is a lesson in love and compassion. It is replacing frustrated impatience with calm amusement and being open to the greatest good for all concerned. In this case, I was grateful that the all-wise mind prevailed.

Love's Masquerade

Carla Sciaky

COLORADO, USA

I cannot understand why I feel so dreadfully upset. Nothing I try is working to soothe it. It's late in the day, and distress is still roiling around within me—and it's growing by the hour. It all started this morning.

This morning, I was sitting with a group of friends, discussing a book we are studying together. We are a close-knit group, having known each other for over twenty years, and the study project is in its fourth year. This particular morning, someone has suggested that we consider a new discussion format.

As each person around the table gave their consent to trying it out on the spot, inexplicably, I found myself descending into an overwhelming panic. Some aspect of the format itself, together with the conversation about the format, was triggering an old wellspring, sucking me and everything in my visual field into a black hole of danger, danger, danger. I had sat in frozen silence, feeling frighteningly defenseless.

Afterward, while driving home, my husband Dan commented that I had been quieter than usual. I attempted to explain to him what I was feeling, which caused me to dissolve into tears. Okay, fine, I thought, maybe crying will release it. But nope, no light bulb, no relief. Normally, I am able to move through this kind of thing by talking with another person. Apparently, this one was tougher than average.

Later, I shared it with a friend over the phone. Out came more. Hearing my own weeping—like the abject heartsick sobs of a lost child—made it clear to me that whatever this had touched was old and deep. I have to admit I now had a new tiny flicker of excitement mixed in with the darkness of the storm, sensing that I might soon be liberated from something. Maybe even Liberated with a capital L.

Tonight, sitting at dinner with Dan, more tears come out, and after dinner, still more. By this time, I am feeling talked out, and knowing I have to do something, I decide to meditate.

I settle myself down into a quiet place, and I choose a guided meditation. In the meditation, he leads me through each energy center, or chakra, of the body while I am encouraged to add a symbol at each one during the process. Healers say that pain comes from blocked energy. Who is blocking it? Me. And what heals me? Love. I choose the mental picture of a red heart as my symbol.

At my third center, my solar plexus immediately following the heart, a giant cartoon-like fat lady appears in my mind. She hugs me, just like the great-aunts from an animated movie of my childhood. The ones that kiss and pinch cheeks and smoosh faces into their ample bosoms where there is a smell of their perfume as well as the food on their aprons, and there is a knowing that they love you to pieces.

I let myself drown in this abundance of adoration because, though I can scarcely breathe while in this embrace, I know this to be a true and important slice of heaven: the messy, sloppy, all-in expression of human love, as unconditional as it can get.

By the time I get to my third eye, I can hardly remember who or where I am. Energy is throbbing throughout my entire body. The meditation instructs me to again conjure up my symbol. It takes a moment to comprehend what is being asked of me. What is that? My what?

And then, it is as if a part of me is running forward like a little kid, down a long corridor, from far away, proclaiming exuberantly, "I found it!!" Now I remember. "Oh, it's LOVE!!" I bring forth the red heart.

In this instant, there is an explosion in my inner universe, like fireworks shimmering and vibrant, delivering my epiphany. It has all been for love. Always. I had loved myself the only way I knew how.

When I was young, all of those things that happened, those things that shouldn't happen to a child yet happen anyway. Things that hurt. Things around which I developed strategies and beliefs that stuck with me and later went awry in my adult years. Those accidents and disappointments that left little—or big—scars, both on the outside and the inside—everything I came up with in response was an act of love for myself, and often my best effort at loving others too.

It is always love, even when it doesn't look like it from the outside. Freezing in fear at the table that morning was my own protection, loving myself in the midst of what felt like a threat. Trying to understand it and explain it to my husband, and later my friend, was my effort to gain clarity, like when my mother used to dig the needle under the surface of my skin to get the splinter out. I was imitating that face of love, trying to coax the source of pain out of my insides.

During the decades that followed my childhood, I was mercilessly critical of myself, scrambling to find solid ground so that I could feel some semblance of safety. Running even from myself in the desperate attempt to cover up and hide what I judged as unacceptable aspects of myself. It was all a misconstrued and convoluted effort to love myself, to receive love from others, and to prove myself worthy of every morsel I could get, both delivering and hoarding the only form of love I knew well—the kind that is carefully masked and hard-won.

Unbeknownst to me, I had in my childhood internalized all the arguing, blaming, judging, worrying, and agonizing as the predominant forms of love that my parents could offer. Some inexplicable wisdom endowed me with a knowing that my parents acted that way because they cared so much. And the truth is I care just as much, both in spite of them and because of them.

The abyss that had cracked open at my feet this morning is serving to be what is delivering me to the doorway of this evening's meditation—climaxing in a private internal lovefest and fireworks show. As if this isn't enough, I am rewarded with a double lesson. Number one: We do it all out of love. Number two: All there is, is love. I am the one who has been distorting it and diverting its flow.

Now, I am the one who is bringing each piece of myself back into the light and learning what it feels like to let Life Force, that energy that is the very source of my existence, reenter these old places—this changes everything.

Priceless Treasures

Janey Holliday
FLORIDA, USA

I find myself driving along I-10, thinking and asking myself questions. Which educational path do I need to take? How can I learn more about my creator and faith? With a troubled soul, I use my time driving to search for answers to my questions. Traveling to my destination, I realize I need guidance, and I whisper to the Infinite One, "Help me."

Several weeks later, on my way back to work after lunch, I am about to pass the Dollar Store, and I hear a still, small voice say, "Stop here." I listen and stop to find the most beautiful roll of royal blue wrapping paper. I begin imagining the bulletin board at work covered with the paper and names of all the Certified Nursing Assistants (CNAs) displayed on the board, recognizing their excellence.

Then something else catches my attention—stars covered with glitter. I mumble, "Wow, I am finding treasures in the Dollar Store!" These silver and gold stars will beautifully accent the bulletin board, and with excitement, I complete my mission. I am ready to zip back to work to decorate the board and spotlight a caring group of CNAs.

The speed of my steps increases as I race to purchase the paper. Noticing a line with one lady at the register, I hurry and stand behind her. I notice a lady in front of me purchasing a royal blue box that matches the color of the paper for the bulletin board. I compliment her on her selection, and I ask her, "What are your plans for the box?"

She replies, "It is for a Queen Esther Ball."

As she leaves the store, I am left thinking about how interesting that sounds, and I wonder what it will involve! I pay for my paper and stars, and as I am walking out of the store, I notice the lady that bought the royal blue box is close by in the parking lot. I walk in her direction, and she introduces herself to me. We chat for a moment, and then she asks if she could gift me a ticket to the Queen Esther Ball. Surprised and filled with joy at her kindness, I accept the ticket.

At the ball, I learn a wealth of information about the story of Queen Esther. As the evening ends and I am leaving the ball, one of the speakers hands me a special bag and asks me to look at it when I return to my room. Later that night, I get comfortable, and I remove a document from the bag. It reads *Honorary Doctorate Degree Application*.

My eyes began to fill with tears, and all I can do is cry tears of joy and amazement at the wonders of the Infinite One. I realize my aching questions are being answered. It just so happens that I have been struggling for the past five years with a decision to either complete a doctorate degree in nursing practice or in theology. On top of that, taking a step to complete a doctorate degree in divinity would require me to spend more time alone with my creator, which is another answer to my heart's longing.

Little did I know that Queen Esther's life would help me understand my purpose in life— to help individuals discover their purpose and design their dreams so they can live a passionate and fulfilling life. And all of these ways of helping others and feeling fulfilled can be summed up into one word—priceless.

A Lifechanging Decision

Pat Acklie-Roth
NEBRASKA, USA

On the outside, it appears I am living the American dream. I've been married for 30 years, own a thriving sewing studio, and live in a beautiful big, old house located near my family. I moved back to the small town of Wausa, Nebraska, 15 years ago to care for my mom after her heart attack. But what starts out as a dream for a good life ends up taking a turn for the worst.

On the inside, I've never been so lonely in my life. I feel unloved, I am the only one present in the marriage, and we have been "roommates" for the last 23 years with separate bedrooms and growing in different directions. When I moved from Florida to take care of my mom, my husband ended up staying behind. Neither of us wants to be the one to file, but we both know it is over.

One of my outlets of hope is an online personal development course that focuses on helping me build my dreams. I realize I deserve so much more from life than I am receiving. As I am going through the course, I start to reevaluate my life. I'm grateful for what I have, and I also want to step even more into a life I love living.

As I sit and do the journaling exercises, I write down about how I would love to have a good, faith-filled husband to worship with. I would love to build a new life, travel, and increase my business revenue. A part of my vision includes my decision to become a certified life coach. With these tools, I can also help other people fulfill their dreams to live a life they love living. I can feel my life changing, and I am looking forward to the future I am creating.

It's a cold December day, and I am making my way to the main floor of the house. As I go down the steps, I lose my balance and fall down my stairs. I am lying there alone and hurting. It is awful. I manage to painfully crawl to the kitchen for my purse, and I make my way out to the garage to my car. I manage to drive to the doctor's office, where he reveals that I have broken my leg and ankle severely.

My brother shows up so he can take me to the hospital for surgery, where they put in a plate and six screws. My sister Sharon calls my husband and reports what's happening and that she is staying with me. My other sister Melva trades off with Sharon back and forth for three weeks until I can stay by myself. If it wasn't for them, I would be in a nursing home! I can't put weight on the foot for three months! And to top it all off, I have no income or financial help from my husband! Not only does he not come to visit me, but he hasn't even called. This confirms that my decision to file is the right one. I am not a failure; I have given my marriage all I could.

It's April now, and I'm back in the studio. I purchase an existing embroidery business, move it in the backroom of my 1,700 square foot building, and double my previous year's revenue.

Dream number one of my vision is fulfilled! And I can feel everything coming together.

It's May 26, and the divorce is final. This chapter is closed, the cloud has lifted, and I am feeling so much happier. I'm freer than I have felt in years. I sleep better, and I wake up happy to start my new day! I love my life now. I love my work and am heavily involved with my church and family. I can now turn my attention to dream number two!

I feel like I have been by myself for the last 15 years already, not married or single! I haven't dated in 30 years. I feel scared to start over and be vulnerable to someone I don't know, especially at 67 years old! What will they expect? Am I too old for this? Will they try to take advantage of me? After all, I have my own business.

My sister-in-law talks me into signing up for an online dating site. I have been going on a couple of those "one date wonders." You know, one date, and you wonder why you are there! I decide that if I am meant to find someone, my Higher Power will send him my way. I have my list of what he has to be like! After a couple of weeks, I give up and cancel my dating site subscription. I decide to let my Higher Power guide the right man to me.

It's almost Friday, and today's my last day to access my dating site. The evening rolls around, and I check my messages one last time. I find myself smiling as I see a notification from John. John messages me, "You have a beautiful smile, and I like your outfit too." I think, okay, why not respond?

We talk for a little while, and he sounds sincere. But I'm very skeptical and don't give out too much information. He is rather nice though, and I would like to talk to him more. He is a widower and lives two hours north of me in Sioux Falls, South Dakota. I tell him my dating site subscription is ending, but if he would like to talk more, he can email me. I am not giving out my phone number or address!

We've been emailing for two weeks now, and it's June. I'm working seven long days a week in the studio on weddings, but I really like what I'm hearing in the emails. We exchange phone numbers, and I decide to meet in another town for a movie at 1 p.m. on Sunday, June 28. The movie is great, and I enjoy his company. So we go for coffee afterward. We have so many things in common. We make our way through two pots of coffee and dinner.

Leaving the restaurant, two gentlemen at the next table tell us, "It's so nice to see such a nice couple so much in love, as you both are!" Our first date and love is showing already! As he walks me to my car, nine hours after meeting, I am thinking I sure hope he kisses me! And he does! What a wonderful day.

Later this year, at Christmas, I get engaged to the man who matches everything on my list. The following April, we get married. All of my dreams came true within a year of making a decision to change my life. I love the life I get to live today.

Living Beyond a Diagnosis

Donna Hornick
CANADA

As I sit there at the hospital, my doctor shares my diagnosis, and I can feel the heaviness behind his words. After my tragic car accident, they are diagnosing me with post-concussion syndrome. They continue explaining, "Your head injury will take two years for it to reverse, and there is no real treatment besides anti-depressant medication." I have never heard of this diagnosis before, so I feel confused about the limited treatment plan.

Some of my symptoms are so uncomfortable. I feel pins and needles as if I have a headband tightly wound around my brain. I also feel extreme anxiety, a foggy mind, and short-term memory loss—which further shoots my anxiety through the roof.

Heading home and back into the swing of things the best I can, I am living day-in and day-out with my foggy thoughts and memory. I am forgetting so many things. There are moments I feel bad because I cannot remember the names of my co-workers who

I have been working with for the past ten years. I am embarrassed and overwhelmed.

Feeling tired and constantly confused, I become frustrated that my doctor has no answers besides putting me on an anti-depressant medication. I can sense the brain fog is causing my problems, not depression, even though I feel a lot of extreme stress and lack of hope.

Revisiting the doctor's office, he addresses my concerns, "The anti-depressant medication will give you some relief for the extreme anxiety you are experiencing."

I try to listen. I ask the doctor, "What about the head pain? And the pins and needles feeling I am experiencing." I have already asked about this a few times by now, hoping for new insight.

He consistently answers with the same statement, "It will take about two or more years to recover."

I think to myself that I need to find a new answer, and I start to obsess with my extreme worry about getting my health back again. I truly feel at a loss for what to do next. At times, I even have suicidal thoughts. I live in silence with it all. It is hard to feel hope when I feel like this is going to be the rest of my life. How can the answer really be that there is nothing I can do but take a pill and wait for two years or more to recover? I feel upset.

Before my appointment is over, I ask my doctor a final question, "Can you explain to me about the two years you talk about? Is it just going to magically go away?"

He replies, "You need to have patience."

As my appointment ends, I feel let down.

While reflecting after my visit to the hospital, my deep intuition gives me a sense, amidst all the anxiety and pain, that this post-concussion syndrome can be resolved in less than two years. I might not have all the details for how, but I know somehow, I am going to find a way to heal myself.

Despite my deep belief in my healing, after four months, I feel even more frustrated and depressed because nothing is changing. I don't even want to leave home. My suicidal thoughts become even louder as it feels this might be the only way to end my pain. This leads me to withdraw and try to commit suicide.

My husband and my children supportively talk to me. They have no idea that I feel this low. Through many tears, I ask, "What else can I do to take away this pain in my brain?" I can sense I am deteriorating quickly, and I can feel myself giving in to my condition.

While doing extensive research on treatments and alternative therapies, one day, I am sitting in my bed, and I loudly demand of the Universe, "I NEED THIS TO CHANGE NOW. I NEED HELP! PLEASE SHOW ME HOW!" I start to watch and listen for the silent whispers.

In this time of distress, I am also teaching a wellness course at a mental health center (where I also feel like I need my own bed, to be honest). While teaching my wellness course, I see a note in my manual about how post-concussion syndrome is listed as a diagnosis for those who can benefit from this course.

I am thinking, "Take your own advice, Donna." And at the same time, I am also shocked. I whisper to myself, "Oh wow, it is a real diagnosis." I can feel this being the beginning of the Universe coming to show me greater possibilities. What if there is more hope than waiting two years?

As more hope starts to set in, my friend calls me a week later, and as we talk and I share my heart, she says she didn't know about what I have been going through. She shares with me about her training in a new modality called Body Talk and offers me a free session. I have never heard of it. I ask her a few questions, and I can feel hope—this might be the answer to my plea for help. "Let's book a session. I need something," I reply out of desperation. I am ready to do whatever it takes to get my health back.

Immediately after my session with my friend, I feel more relaxation in my brain. I can feel things starting to shift! Even a little bit means a lot to me at this point. This hope leads me to book more sessions. After a few more sessions, my pins and needles are completely gone. Yes, they are GONE! Relief pours over me, and I can feel my life weaving itself back together.

The new longing in my heart is now to keep believing as I continue to see my outlook and symptoms change. I am so grateful. So grateful. With this feeling of joy, I say, "Thank you, Universe, for having my back." When I began trusting, my answers came within a couple of weeks after making the demand. Clarity is power. After four or five more sessions, I decide to take courses in Body Talk, and I become certified. This is the beautiful beginning of finding myself and helping others do the same.

Gifts from the Darkness

Mandy Morris
AUSTRALIA

Standing outside of a classroom at the Adult Education College, I am crying uncontrollably. The floodgates have opened up, and I can't stop. My nose is running, and I have no tissues. Snot is seeping down my face, mixing with my tears. I think back to telling my young son that tears are precious, like jewels. Well, they certainly don't feel like that right now. I wipe my nose on my sleeve. I look like a mess, but I am beyond caring—lost in my own misery. My life is unraveling before my eyes, and I don't have the strength to keep up the pretense that "It's all good."

I have been running from this moment for months now. Deep down, I know that it was going to catch up with me eventually. It's time to face my dark night. To look it squarely in the face. My seemingly empty future lies before me, and I am scared to feel the enormity of my loss. My stoic wall is crumbling.

My partner of 11 years, the father to our almost ten-year-old son, had decided to step away from our lives to go back to England

and find himself. He is nearing 60 and is going through a belated midlife crisis. He tells me that it's nothing personal, and he still loves me. I might have been able to stomach this more easily if he had the courtesy to leave our son and me some kind of support, but he didn't. Out of sight, out of mind.

I don't remember exactly what emotion I felt first when he told me. But today, my emotions dance between sadness and anger. I don't mind the anger so much; at least, that had some fire and energy to it. It's the sadness that I am afraid of—like a bottomless pit draining my life force. I know for the sake of my son, I can't afford to go there. I must resist the strong pull of deep melancholy and depression that is calling my name.

I become a master of distraction and keep myself busy. I get creative and find ways to pay the bills. I take in housemates, such as hosting Japanese students, and do AirBnB. At one stage, I have so many tenants that my son and I are sleeping in tents in the backyard.

Then one day, seemingly out of the blue, the ultimate distraction presents itself—a charity cycle trip down the coast of South India. It begins innocently enough. I am sitting at an unfamiliar café, sipping on a soy latte while totally engrossed in an article about a fundraising cycle tour. As I sit, sip, and read, a polite young man introduces himself to me. It turns out he is the cycle tour leader, and he lets me know, "There are only two spots left to participate." I know in an instant that those places have my son's and my name on them.

I get home and quickly put down the deposit to secure our spots. I am excited for the first time in months. I feel alive. It's the next day when the fear kicks in. I don't have the finances to go off traveling, let alone come up with extra money to support a charity. I must be some kind of crazy!

By deciding that we are doing this and keeping my focus on the vision of India and the good I can do, ideas start flowing in for the financial means to make it happen. Not only do we raise the funds for the charity and cycle over 270km, after the tour, my son and I spend another six weeks traveling independently, exploring this wild and wonderful country.

Getting back home to Australia, I soon discover that the dark night isn't finished with me. With no distractions, my everyday reality hits me. And I lose my old job. With no income, no partner, and no prospects, my depression looms like a dementor from Harry Potter, threatening to suck out the last of my joy. I can't let this happen. I have a son to care for.

So, against the grain, I do what I have to and enroll in a Certificate 3 in Disability Support. This is where you find me at the beginning of the story. Outside the classroom, crying uncontrollably. It's not that the course was that bad, a little uninspiring perhaps. It's what it represents: the last departure from my old life.

Fast track forward. The student most likely to drop out (me) finds herself a job in a day center supporting people living with a disability. It turns out it suits me. I can be myself and share all that I am, including spontaneous outbursts of song with my ukulele and creative play. Reconnecting with my love for life awakens in me the desire for more. The Universe is indeed conspiring for me to keep growing.

Like my trip to India, this comes in the form of a seemingly random set of circumstances. I fly down to Sydney to celebrate a friend's 60th Birthday. She has kindly put me up on her living room floor, where she has lovingly piled numerous thin mattresses on top of each other. It is very uncomfortable, and I can't sleep. So, I get my phone out, put my earbuds in so as not to disturb my friend in her small apartment, and find myself totally absorbed in a master class coming from the States.

This is the moment I find my mentor. As the old saying goes, "When the student is ready, the teacher appears." Well, I am ready. This is no accident. By 7:00 a.m., despite having sworn to myself that I would never study again after the dryness of my last training, I have signed up, and I am on my way to becoming a certified transformational life coach.

This is a reminder that I am far more powerful than any circumstance or condition that I can ever go through. The dark night is inevitable to show up at some point. I couldn't avoid this situation. But there are jewels to be found here. I am so grateful for all of the growth and learning my dark time has gifted me. And to see the light at the end of the tunnel.

The Investment

Margaret Evanow
CALIFORNIA, USA

I can hardly contain my swelling emotions. I am on my way. My consultant has found a way for me to join a spiritually oriented training program so I can start my career as a coach. It looks like I will be extending the payments to get signed up, but I make the decision anyway. This is important to me. And I will find a way to make the payments!

I lay my claim of faith that it will all work out, and I make the down payment. I'm in! The consultant celebrates with me and gives me the details on what comes next. We say our goodbyes, and the call ends.

I am surrounded by silence. I can hear ringing in my ears, and my brain starts to buzz. "What have I done?" I ask myself out loud. I can't make these payments! The excitement, hope, and exuberant feelings about investing in myself and my personal growth turn swiftly into a jolt of panic! I start to feel a burning in my chest. My breaths are coming fast—like I can't get air.

Wild voices in my mind start to nay-say and screech. This is it. I am going down! I am falling into darkness. I try to steady myself. My heart is beating too fast! Breathe, Margaret! Breathe! I struggle to hold on to my former exuberance while barely being able to remember how I just felt while saying YES to myself—to investing in growth and expansion.

I feel a wave of tsunami-size panic sweep over me! I feel my grip on my former feelings and hopes slip away. I am alone. Alone with my terror, yes, not fear, but T-E-R-R-O-R! A part of me shouts, "What have you done? No one can help you out of this! Now you've gone too far!" I know the commitment I agree to requires a financial stream I do not have. There is no wiggle room in my budget. I have had the same income for over 15 years.

My fear starts to increase even further, and I start to spiral. I only have so much coming in every month. What have I done? This decision is going to end with me in collections! The hot tears follow my icy chills of fear. I shake with fear, crying loudly. I sink into my old way of thinking about how I never have enough.

Finally, I reach complete exhaustion after giving in to the fear. I again experience silence. After what feels like hours, I can almost hear a small, quiet voice. My voice? I am not sure. But I listen, and I receive the message: "Margaret, this is what you want, and you need this to grow." Harsh voices rally against this quiet truth. But again, that quiet and assuring voice within me speaks. "You are worth taking this step towards your freedom." A sharp and angry voice in my mind asks, "How?"

In the silence, I listen again. "This is your time; you need to do this. You know how to do this. Remember, you have done this before. You know how." I calm my terrors. I slow my breathing. I wipe my tears and blow my nose. As I take a deep and centering breath, I pick up my schedule to look at the days I have kept open. I shiver at the "just enough" for bills schedule I keep, and I listen again for comfort. My breathing is the only sound I hear for a moment.

In an unfamiliar place within me, I land on the solid ground of KNOWING, with unwavering belief, that this will work out. With my client schedule open on my lap, I request out loud, "Fill it. I am willing to do what I need to do. Please, fill it." My heart opens with this simple but confident appeal. I rearrange my schedule to maximize my open time slots for clients. I am filled with gratitude for the clients who will fill these gaps in my schedule.

I smile as I continue to reassure myself that if I build it, they will come! I create an inviting and open space for new clients to enter. Calm and grounded in my truth—ask and you will receive.

My Infinity Year

Deborah A. Servetnick

MARYLAND, USA

My colleagues and I watch nervously as the auditorium lights, suspended on their half-century-old cables, sway above our heads. This is an earthquake nobody saw coming.

In Baltimore, it's the "Back-to-School Week for Teachers." The type of week with too many meetings like this one, and all we really want is to prepare our classrooms. Amidst the chaos, we file out to call our own children who have been enjoying these last days of summer vacation. But all of us come to the same realization—there's no cell service.

By the weekend, the hurricane arrives, most of Baltimore is out of power, and I have no electricity where I live. The new school year is getting ready to start after a two-day delay. Excitement and terror have always tagged along for my first day of class with my high school students. And it is about to begin.

I wake up drenched in sweat from the lack of air conditioning. I shower and get dressed in the dark. My hair is in a ponytail, and I decide to skip the makeup. I arrive at 7:00 a.m. to greet my students, and by the end of the day, I can barely stand. Was it the eight hours in a 94-degree Fahrenheit classroom? Maybe it's all of those days at home without power, no AC, barely sleeping, and stressing about everything. I have vertigo, yet it's the first week of school. There's no way I can call out.

The next day is so bad I can't remember how I just drove home. I decide to call in and take a sick day, even though I am feeling immensely guilty and horribly inadequate. Thankfully, lying flat on my back gives me relief. Lying here on my bed, I remember a favorite stress-melting tool I used over and over as a massage therapist and energy healer before I went back to school for my master's degree in education. I rely on my Jin Shin Jyutsu #22 acupressure points—two sets of three fingers up from the nipple line. And while I am doing this, this is how I find the lump in my breast.

"We're moving. I gave notice. There's still no AC, but he lets the guy on the top floor run his generator right by our open windows," my husband shares.

"What did you say?" I call from the bed to my husband. The generator is loud.

"We're moving in December when our lease is up."

"Good, December. Because you know once school starts, I can't do anything, nothing, until Christmas break."

He responds, "We move December 1st. Our lease is up on November 30th."

I reiterate, "No, that can't happen. I can't pack and move between now and then. There's no way."

My husband replies, "That's what it is. I already gave notice. It's done."

After a few weeks, I get my biopsy results during Rosh Hashana.

Rosh Hashana is my favorite holiday—a celebration. The start of the new year! My 53rd birthday was eight days after that, Yom Kippur. The day of At-Onement. All summer, I was excited for this birthday because it's an eight year. The infinity year. My best birthdays have always been "eight years"!

Like when I was 26 and had a thriving bodywork practice in Philadelphia, 35 when I moved to a beautiful studio to do bodywork in a hipster neighborhood, and 44 when I completed my master's degree, was promoted from teacher to an administrative position at a Philly alternative school, was engaged to Donnie, and made plans to move to Baltimore.

And now, here is 53. We are moving without a place to live lined up. Fighting stage 3 cancer and getting very sick, very fast. But really, the chemo, not the cancer, is killing me. What keeps me going is hearing my mother and other people who have passed on speak to me, reassuring me that everything will turn out fine as I make it through these mind-bending nights after chemo. I can see spirits all over the bedroom.

My husband is lying next to me, holding my hand while I tell him what I am hearing and seeing. Donnie and my daughter Emanuelle take the best care of me. They cook me miso soup, help me in every way, and tiptoe around so as not to wake me up. But something strange is starting to happen. I can hear the words spoken on the TV in the next room, even though I've been deaf in one ear since childhood, so I typically use closed captions and turn up the volume relentlessly.

My reconnection to spirit makes everything easier emotionally while everything in the physical world is disintegrating. My job is my family's link to our health insurance, but I can't walk, type, find words—all side effects from chemo. Teaching isn't an option. Up until cancer, I never got sick, so I had purchased the most inexpensive coverage offered.

I discover why our coverage is so cheap after my health plan doesn't approve an ultrasound to monitor the growth of the tumor while they turn up the chemo dosage. I am giving myself injections that I have to prefill into syringes, so my health plan can save money. I am overdosed on chemo so my insurance provider can cut my doctor visits in half. A mastectomy is scheduled with a general surgeon, not a breast surgeon. My girlfriends are concerned. I want a second opinion. I want new doctors.

Amidst all of this, we find and buy the perfect house for us so we can move in December to a great neighborhood with good schools. My husband, the most patient and loving man I've ever known, answers all of the questions, checks the boxes, and we get our mortgage. I don't have to go to my job; I can use my sick days and miracle sick bank of my teachers' association.

From an apartment we love, we move into a house with trees outside every window, a tennis court, a playground, and the rolling green of ballfields. And now it is time to sell my childhood piano. I brought this piano with me from my mother's house to Baltimore. But it's time to let it go. It doesn't fit in our new home.

It turns out my growing dissatisfaction with my health plan during open enrollment is a gift. With two days left and my bald head, I turn in paperwork for a new plan. However, it will be a month before the plan takes effect. I get the best breast surgeon, a local legend, and pay out of pocket for everything, trusting it is all working out.

Dr. Schultz orders an ultrasound, and he sends me to a new oncologist, who approves my medical cannabis. I am grateful for my new medical team as I try not to think about the bills I am racking up. I accept a deal for the piano and thank my mother for watching over me.

The piano's new owners arrive with their piano movers as I am shutting our mailbox in the lobby. They are so happy to buy my piano for their young son who is starting piano lessons. I am glad someone will enjoy my piano. Noticing I keep my hat on, the mom buying the piano smiles, and she hands me a small pile of cash.

I breathe deeply after counting the money. In my hand, I am holding the exact amount listed on my bill for my ultrasound.

Clouds to Dreams

Theresa Garvin
MASSACHUSETTS, USA

My husband Tim and I are moving from Connecticut to Massachusetts. Soon after we arrive and start our new jobs, we have our first daughter, Meghan. We end up buying a house in Maynard to settle in with our new family.

Two years later, we have our second daughter, Erin. Our family is growing, and we enjoy building a family. Top it off with our beautiful Chesapeake Bay Retriever named Maggie, and our life feels complete. There were some important steps along the way to get to this point though. Here's how it went the year before I became pregnant with Erin.

After having Meghan, I am hired as a school social worker in Lowell, and I think I have nailed the best mother's job out there! Good pay through the union, school and summer vacations, lots of paid holidays, and off work by 3:00 p.m. How much better can it get?

There is one thing that I didn't plan on—how difficult the

daycare coordinating would become. Before long, I begin to notice a pattern. As each year comes and goes, one of our daughters ends up being incredibly unhappy in their daycare. Within two years, we have switched daycare centers three times because of this issue.

This particular year, Erin feels so unhappy at daycare that she cries every day and clings to me, begging me to stay. I end up having to pass her off to a childcare worker as I dash off to my job. Most days, I cry on my way to work, as I am riddled with guilt because I feel like a horrible mother.

A few more years go by, and I decide to quit my job in order to stay home for a year so I can be with our daughters. We both want our kids to be happier. After I quit my job, we find out a little surprise. I am pregnant with Colin. We are thrilled and scared at the same time about having a third child. This means I will have another year at home.

Colin has just celebrated his first birthday after we move into our new home in Sudbury. Two weeks later, he gets sick, and we are rushed by ambulance to Children's Hospital, where Colin spends the next five days in the intensive care unit. This is the worst experience of my life, as Colin's life is at risk, and they tell us that he may have died had we not brought him in today. He is diagnosed with ketoacidosis. This can occur when blood sugars are too high over a long period of time, which can result in a diabetic coma and ultimately death.

There is no question that both Tim and I are traumatized and sleep-deprived and now scared beyond belief as we have no idea about how to care for a one-year-old with diabetes.

My new full-time job becomes about learning how to keep our one-year-old son alive with insulin. I administer 8-10 finger pricks per day, along with shots after each time he eats. Tim and I are both anxious because we feel unqualified and hope for the best. I am living in constant fear that Colin will die from a mistake I make with his insulin.

The following summer, after Colin's second birthday, our house is struck by lightning during a storm that comes out of nowhere. We get out safely; however, much of our home is destroyed in the fire, so we move into a rental home for six months while the contractors rebuild our home.

So here I am. A young mother, still new to town and knowing almost nobody, and I have to care for our three kids: one with a chronic medical condition and two others with ADHD. And now we are living in a rental home. This is NOT the life I had imagined. This feels more like a nightmare, and one that I am starring in.

After the fire, I feel a constant black cloud hanging over me— one that follows me everywhere. I am depressed, isolated, scared, and stuck! As neighbors introduce me to someone, the person I meet will often say, "Oh, I heard about you. You're the one who has the baby with diabetes and the house that got struck by lightning. That sounds so awful." It is awful. I feel like everyone pities us. I pity us! I somehow feel like I have failed miserably as a mother, and I feel hopeless.

Once we moved back to our fixed-up home, I start to search for the perfect daycare that will be willing and able to care for a three-year-old with diabetes. I decide to try the local daycare cooperative that many mothers in town have raved about. This is a daycare that I will also need to work at, as that is how cooperatives work.

So, I happily enroll Colin, thinking it's the perfect plan because I get to train the teacher in how to do finger pricks, and I will be there some of the time while training other parents and helping out.

Six weeks later, Colin develops separation anxiety and begs me not to go back to the cooperative. I am also unhappy with Colin being there as I notice that his teacher has been avoiding talking to me about how to manage his diabetes, and it is so much work to explain the protocol to every parent. Parents look scared and overwhelmed during the times I explain how to monitor Colin's blood sugars.

I suddenly realize that we are paying for a daycare that he hates, and that is adding more stress to our lives. Not less stress. I sense that ominous cloud still hanging over me.

It is at this point that I decide to deeply listen to Colin's voice of fear and unhappiness, and then I listen to my own still, small voice. I think about how many daycare struggles we have already been through. I acknowledge how I always feel like I have to try to adjust and have our kids adjust to the daycare centers rather than the other way around.

I make a bold move by going to the director of the cooperative, insisting we be given a full refund as I am taking our son out of the program. She explains, "We have never given refunds before, and it's against our policy."

I reply, "You could not provide the level of care our son had been promised, and we should not pay for a service you never delivered."

The cloud begins to lift after this exchange, as we are given a full refund, and our son is enrolled in a preschool program that he falls in love with. They have a full-time nurse who has ample years of experience in working with children with diabetes, and I can have peace of mind to go back to work. I find a great job, and I am able to gradually build up my hours. Making this bold decision is my first step in creating a life that I truly love living!

Just Call Joan

Penny Richichi
CALIFORNIA, USA

My job is becoming increasingly less enjoyable. Tensions are high between management and staff, and one by one, my co-workers are leaving for other jobs. I am torn. I love my work, but the tensions grow each week.

As I drive to work on a Monday morning, tears are streaming down my face at the thought of another workweek. Something inside of me loudly says, "NOW." I know this "NOW" means it is time for me to leave too. Instantly, I feel relief, and I submit my resignation during my day at work.

On the drive home that evening, I notice the relief is still there, but it fluctuates now with another powerful emotion—fear. Unlike my colleagues who left before me, I don't have another job lined up. It's time to get a plan in place. I update my resume, research available job opportunities, and start practicing answers to common interview questions.

As I begin to actively search, I notice I am unsettled. I get curious about this. What I discover is that my heart is yearning for an opportunity to "test drive" a position. It's important to me that the next position I accept is not simply a match for my skills but that the organization's culture is a match as well. I want a collaborative environment.

Once I discover this, I begin to research available temporary and temporary-to-hire positions. This is the best way to "test drive" a position, right? The challenge I come across is that nothing I find at that point is of interest or a match for my skills.

While running errands one day, I happen to notice my friend Joseph driving down the opposite side of the road. I haven't seen him in quite some time! We pull over to exchange hellos.

During our brief conversation, he tells me about his new job and how he is thrilled with his new position as the director of a local non-profit program within a larger organization. His excitement is apparent for his position, the program, and the larger organization. He asks what I have been up to, and I give him a short synopsis, including that I have tendered my resignation.

He immediately says, "I want you to call my friend Joan. She's the director of another program within the same organization, and they want to hire someone immediately. You would be a perfect fit!" Upon hearing more about the position, I am definitely intrigued. Yet, there is one obvious major drawback. It is a permanent position.

I thank Joseph for the lead, but I tell him I am quite resolved that I don't want a permanent position at this time. Joseph continues, "I will call her as soon as I get home and tell her about you. All you have to do is follow up. Just call Joan!"

As I drive home, his words echo in my mind to just call Joan. I decide to take action even though it doesn't appear that it will be what I want. It's simply a phone call though. I will give Joseph the courtesy of following up.

I call Joan the next morning. Joan's first words to me are, "Penny, Joseph told me about you, and we'd love for you to submit your resume. First, I want to let you know, it is important for us to find a good match for this position, and we need someone right away to perform the job. So, the board and I are making the decision to hire someone for three months.

"After three months, we will re-advertise the position and hire someone for the permanent position. There is no guarantee that the person who is hired for the three-month position will be chosen for the permanent one, but of course, they would be most welcome to apply for it." This is what I need to hear.

I immediately apply for the three-month position, and I get the job. After three months, I reapply for the permanent position, and I get that job too. It is the collaborative environment I was longing for. The ancient poet Rumi said, "What you seek is seeking you." What I was seeking was indeed seeking me.

New York, New York

Yasmina Rauber
SWITZERLAND

The plane touches down on American soil, and I breathe again—the first full deep breath since I left Geneva, Switzerland. And now, here I am in New York, 23 years old, and ready for a brand-new start. Everyone scrambles to their feet to grab their bags from the overhead lockers. I sit in my chair while I wait for the rush to cool down.

I have waited a long time to make this journey. It took working long hours, saving every last bit of my money I could, and planning for everything until the early hours. And now here I am, feeling stuck to my seat—afraid of what is on the other side of the plane door. Afraid that I might be making the biggest mistake of my life. Who do I think I am to believe that I can make it in New York City? I have no qualification to be a stockbroker! I am an experienced tradeshow organizer!

I left home on a bad note, so I only brought my clothes and a few books. No good luck charms, no talismans, and no help from my parents. They told me, and anyone who would listen, that I am making the biggest mistake of my life and that I won't amount to much.

The door opens with a rush of hot air, and everyone starts filing out. As I stand at the top of the steps, I again breathe in deeply. "New York City, here I come!" I announce, more as a persuasion to myself than the brave proclamation it sounds like to everyone around me.

Next, I arrive at the Martha Washington Hotel for women, where a room has been booked by my new employer for my first few nights in New York. It's located in the lower eastside, not a nice area.

After a week, I finally dial Mae's number. Mae has known our family since we were children and is a real New Yorker. She knows every corner of it and loves every bit of it. As she realizes where I am staying, she immediately orders me to pack up my things, and she picks me up. I get to stay at her place for a few days, and this gives me time to find a decent place to live.

"Next week, I'll introduce you to Elly. She might have a room for rent." I can't wait to start my new job. I am lined up to begin as a stockbroker trainee the following week, and everything seems to be falling into place. A new life, and far away from the expectations and disappointments in Geneva. I am about to start truly living!

Elly Sternberg is an old, extravagant-looking Hungarian living in exclusive Sutton Place on the East River. She is everything I imagined a glamorous old New Yorker would be. She wears stunning bright-colored clothes and black leather pants and is dripping with jewelry. Her apartment is full of overstuffed sofas, mountains of books, and there are curios and trinkets on every surface. She fascinates me from the very first moment I lay my eyes on her. She is looking for someone to keep her company and at a reasonable price for rent. I jump at the chance! What a find! A great location, private bathroom, meals, and stories of the old days to entertain me. But I soon realize things aren't turning out how I expected.

To prove my parents wrong, I begin to work in earnest and train for long hours at my new job. I learn how to trade Eurobonds, and I discover I am really good at it. But I am paid a pittance for all of the hours I put in. I am so tired at the end of the day that I hardly have a social life, except on the weekends.

We go to nice restaurants like Ai Cantinori, I Tre Merli, or the Brasserie. We entertain guests at Katz's for pastrami sandwiches and have high tea at the Russian Tea Room. By the time the Eurobonds trade stops, I am burnt out and bored. My soul isn't in it. Elly has always worked long hours, and her work ethic quickly rubs off on me. "Living it up can wait," she tells me.

One day, Elly decides to move to Spain. Luckily, at this same time, an old friend from school in Geneva is studying nearby in New York, and she happens to be looking for a roommate! So, I go from 54th and Sutton Place South to 84th Street and 3rd Avenue. It's a studio, but it's a penthouse with an amazing view! Our place is almost a makeshift hotel. Every other week, someone else is staying with us.

At the same time as I move, I am approached by an ex-colleague who is starting their company, and they want to hire me. My income doubles just like that! This new flow of money allows me to breathe a bit more and enjoy the Big Apple!

As Christmas arrives, I need to leave the studio because a few friends from Pascale are coming to stay in our studio for the holidays. Again, I am lucky because Nick is returning to Switzerland for the holidays, and he is kind enough to lend me his room. He doesn't return to NYC, and we agree on a payment arrangement.

This goes on for six months. Here I am on 77th street between Lexington and 3rd in a beautiful, fully-furnished, two-bedroom, and two-bathroom apartment! But it doesn't stop there. In fact, James is so happy with our very pleasant cohabitation that he asks me to stay longer under the same terms. And on the job side, I am also lucky! After the stockbroker company filed a Chapter 11, a friend of mine hires me.

So, despite having no qualifications, dreaming BIG, getting in an uncomfortable place of jumping into the unknown, by putting the actions in place, and by trusting the Universe that if I want to stay in NYC, there would be a way. I managed to find three jobs and three nice homes over the course of three years. To this day, these were certainly the most difficult times, but also the very best years of my life!

Blessings Amidst Life's Storms

Faiana Makahununiu Brown

UTAH, USA

I thought I would be further along in my life by now, and I wonder if I am successful in the things that don't really matter. This is my reality as I think about life today. I am 15 days away from hitting my 51st birthday. I am on track to being able to live the life of success I have been dreaming about for the past 18 years. At the same time, I am at a crossroads in my life as I face two diverging opportunities—one that provides me success and freedom, and another path that leads to purpose and fulfillment. Let me recap on what led to this moment, though, about ten months earlier.

It's 2020, and I am starting off the year differently than most people facing the COVID pandemic. I am being offered an executive vice president position at a new network marketing company that will give me the opportunity to develop leaders, design a marketing system that will provide the ordinary person a platform to first believe in themselves, and obtain time and money freedom by leveraging the efforts, talents, and money of others for a common dream.

In return, the company will compensate me with a monthly salary, weekly commission on group sales, and 3% of the company's annual profits. I will have the freedom to work from anywhere and choose my work hours. As I say yes to this position and dream, I realize in my heart and mind that the past 18 years in the direct sales industry have finally paid off.

Flash forward ten months. Here I am, faced with the decision between success and freedom vs. purpose and fulfillment. There's the old saying, "You either build the life of your dreams, or someone will hire you to build theirs."

My awakening is on November 3, 2020, when I realize that *I* am hired by someone to build their dream. During the last nine months, with all the skills I have acquired from climbing to the top levels of various network marketing companies, I have poured my heart and soul into creating a system that is simple and easy to replicate. Thousands of dollars and countless hours are invested in attending seminars to help better understand why people do what they do and how to build people up, who in turn build businesses.

I take time, the most valuable commodity, away from spending it with those I love the most to ensure that the system and culture I am building will weather any storm that most network marketing companies can face. I have full control of the direction the company is going. What I fail to investigate is the heart and vision the CEO has.

At the end of October, I am informed that the focus will shift from developing and building people to driving sales to increase revenue for the company. The system, culture, and commitment to the people that I empowered are now removed, and I am instructed to follow the new system and vision the CEO has, or I will be asked to leave.

I feel betrayed, insignificant, unappreciated, and worthless as I realize what I have given up personally to help build this dream network marketing company. What most people don't know is that I told my husband to take a year off of work to begin making memories with our son. My husband, Gerald Liti Brown, missed out on our daughter's life because he was working 16-18 hours a day in order to give our children the opportunities and resources to live their dreams, something that he didn't get to have.

If I follow my heart and am true to who I am by leaving my position, my family will be left without a source of income to provide for the necessities of life. If I follow the vision and plans of the CEO, my family will have more than enough for necessities and experiences; however, I will lose my purpose and fulfillment. I will lose myself.

Someone once told me, "Not all storms come to disrupt your life. Some come to clear your path." For three days, I struggle with the options I am facing. It is not a win/win, but a lose/lose. One right choice I have made in my life is choosing Gerald Liti Brown as my husband. He knows that something is heavy on my mind and heart, and it isn't just the work situation but more related to my spirit. I finally have the courage to share the struggle of my soul.

My husband's response is one that I didn't expect. Without blinking an eye, he asks, "What do you want to do?"

I hesitantly say, "I don't want to stay, but we will not have any income. I don't know what we can do for income during a pandemic, and everyone is struggling financially."

He responds, "Hon, I believe in you, I love you, and most importantly, I want you to be happy. Don't worry about the finances because we will figure it out as we always have."

This taught me that I can often limit the opportunity to truly live a life I would absolutely love. A life of success, of time and money freedom coupled with fulfillment and purpose. The key is to not focus on the obstacles but instead to focus on the desire. I take the steps that I desire, and I say no to the CEO's vision. And I say yes to mine.

Only days after making my decision, I am contacted by a consultant from a life coaching institute, and I make the decision to enroll. My husband sells his new ATV in order to have the down payment for my life coaching certification. A month later, I am approached with an opportunity to be a part of a network marketing company where the focus is developing people and building a business with spiritual success principles, one that focuses on the individual and not the sales volume.

My husband and I are now business partners with this network marketing company, and best of all, we are surrounded by like-minded individuals.

My mother has been known to tell me, "Don't get so caught up making a living that you forget to make a life." I am so happy and grateful for where I am today as I work with my husband on building our business together and seizing every moment to live intentionally for excellence.

Metamorphosis

Ellen T. Reed

TEXAS, USA

In 2010, I looked into the mirror, not liking the woman staring back at me. I was the heaviest I have ever been, and although I loved my daughters more than anything else in the world, I could not love myself. One day, I would feel beautiful and wonderful, while another day, I felt like an unorganized slob who didn't want to clean the house. I could see the pieces of an ideal life scattered around me, but only two of them seemed to fit together and click for me—being a loving mother and a crafter.

The rest of the pieces seemed to be adequate to form the picture of a life any woman would desire, yet something was missing from the picture. How could I have felt more love and confidence in my marriage? Where was the reassurance that I could feel loved for who I am?

I guess I was in the caterpillar stage of my life; there was almost enough sustenance to fill my personal needs, but there was no beauty, just energy food. Only survival. Sometimes it was difficult to find food, and I felt responsible for providing the family food budget. But I was barely working.

My babies received their needs before I fulfilled my own. I knew that if I kept feeding my babies love and nutrition, they would thrive emotionally and physically. And they did. After graduating high school with honors and then college with aspirations of serving in healthcare, this Momma caterpillar had provided a full life for her babies.

In 2017, it was time to crawl into the chrysalis. I was now divorced, and I sent my last baby to college. She prepared for the next chapter of her life—a move to Texas. Spending precisely a year in this cocoon stage, sending love to my babies over twenty-six hundred miles away, I prepared to evolve into my new home state.

Inside my cocoon, I grew wings by learning that my marriage was not my fault, but instead a missed awareness in the Papa caterpillar. My wing colors seemed to grow brighter; I was beautiful all along; he just needed to dull my colors to make his shine brighter. Papa was not attracted to me but instead had been using our marriage to hide his truth.

I could feel my wings start to flutter inside the chrysalis, but I knew there was more to occur before emerging from my cramped quarters. There was the discomfort of trying to fit a classroom teacher's mold under the critical eye of a distrusting principal. I knew that I was not too fond of first-grade teaching, as these children did not understand the school social structure.

On one cramped day of growth, I placed my hand on a child's knee to keep him seated during a class lesson, but he told his parents that I walloped him. The distrusting principal terminated my role as a substitute teacher. The emersion from the chrysalis was quite the battle. Due to this stressful loss, I found myself in a terrifying hydroplaning accident that nearly claimed my life. Somehow with two angels protecting me, I walked out of the accident without a scratch.

Thus, the emersion from the chrysalis was successful. How do I know? Within one week of the accident and a short prayer to my higher power asking for guidance, I happened upon a podcast with a wonderful and soothing woman, with the voice of an angel, promoting her inspirational book. I remember reading the book in five days and signing up for a pivotal program.

By April, I am a member of this extraordinary family of positive, supportive people. I have a crystal-clear dream to create a log cabin enrichment center for families. These families will learn more about each other and get the opportunity to grow stronger together.

In October, I am now driving confidently to a Dallas conference to meet my new best friends and the woman with the angelic voice. Six weeks before this conference, an email had arrived from this wonderful woman requesting individuals who went through the program to create a short video of what it meant to them. I wasn't sure my butterfly wings were ready for a video, so I made a digital scrapbook copy as a gift to present to her personally.

As I arrive at the conference, I quickly realize it is going to be a challenge for me. In a large group of people, I mask my social awkwardness. I have learned to be in front of the crowd, even if it means that I show up hours before an event. For me, the best seat is an end seat on the aisle that allows a direct sightline to the speaker. Although I have been creating these personal comfort skills all of my life, I hadn't known that these skills revealed that I am on the autism spectrum.

Luckily, I had bought a ticket to attend the Wisdom Lunch, a lunch with a reduced number of attendees who can ask this earthly angel questions. I raise my hand, but I am not chosen so I can present the gift. At the end of the lunch, I beeline for her son because I know he can take the book to her.

I fully expect him to thank me and head into the auditorium, but what comes next surpasses my greatest desire. He turns his full attention to me and opens the book I had created to present to his mother. His jaw drops when I tell him why I made it. Instead of thanking me with the book in hand, he escorts me to the auditorium ahead of the crowd.

Here I am on the first day of my first conference, and I am getting a private introduction to my living angel. The woman who changed my life one hundred and eighty degrees in eight short months!

After my mentor's son introduces me to her, I explain the gift to her. And I am thinking what a thrill it is to meet my mentor privately to present my dream! She shares with me that very few people have this amount of clarity before attending this conference, but I don't realize that.

My heart is full of joy. This conference is everything I imagined and more! And after the conference is all said and done, I realize something valuable. I can smile today at the happy woman in the mirror whose life is continually changing as I use new tools to walk closer to my enrichment center and my dream. I feel almost as if I could spread my wings to fly.

A Sweet Little Story About a Sweet Little Girl

Veslemøy Sæther Olavsbråten

NORWAY

There is a lady. The lady is me.
She lives in a house ordinarily.
With husband and daughter
running and living
like people do
giving and giving

The summer goes by
and leaves start to fall
A new little baby
in a belly is born

A long time later
the baby grows
into the life
only mummy knows

There is this mum. This mum is me.
Lives with the belly
how good it can be!
feeling ordinarily

Life seeking
the expression of
life
throughout the baby
with peace
and cry

Winter goes over
spring blinks hello
a mum is waiting
for the belly to go
into a baby keeping tight
belly to baby
sleepless nights

It is some toxicity
connection by blood
a baby in danger
doctors tell

Should I be worried?
cause I am not
I know the baby
is at a perfect spot

Between life and life
in my belly sweet
toxicity grows
a danger beat

The last month is crazy
they want her out
the sweet little baby
a little sprout

Deep in my being
A whisper to wait
tell doctors don't!
it will go great

there is a true meaning
behind all the scenes
let it work,
feel it beam
the little and true
behind all the scenes

I trust the gut feel
doctors agree
protect and watch
pictures on screens

little by little
I know in my heart
the baby is healthy
give it a start!

I learn that all choices
are choices to make
doctors, professionals
for everyone's sake
scared in choices
is losing the mark
this is new to them
to wait for the start

I know I want
a safe holy birth
and holy to me?
a sacred work

A midwife I trust
home birth so safe
I want to have
this choice to take

But doctors tell
it is not safe at all
find a hospital place
to run that ball

I trust the feeling
deep in my gut
to trust in the process
and find my luck

A Saturday morning
in the very spring sun
I feel that my belly
is working a run

But no pain too much,
exactly the way
it knows the best path
from the big greater fray

A long day of working
at ordinary things
I need some sleep
and from nothing it brings

a holy birth blooming
that has to be true
before Monday morning
will prove it to blue

Sunday
the earliest
woke up so fast
my belly is hurting
understanding the grasp

All so close
to come
to pass

the very best hours
a walk into life
the freedom is ours
husband and wife

out in the morning
the horse walks with me
into the morning
walking her free!

both of us know:
walk it through!
just believe it,
a heart fire lit

We walk the slow horse walk
her calm trust in life
knowing to support me
is gifted wise

two hours later
our daughter is born
in the room
right there
beyond
a simple front door

Many shocked faces
the ambulance came
the midwife and all
nothing to blame

nine people total
only to see
that this little baby
has come to be

a healthy sweet baby
a healthy sweet smile
a lady to mother
in the hours of night

A perfect little
coming to life
the belly and baby
United by sight

Sitting so calmly
a newborn in hands
nursing my baby
Perfect it stands

walking us out
In the fresh summer air
Sunrise shines
into water drops swear
memories telling a story
the spectacular honesty of glory

the rooster
brings us back to earth
cock-a-doodle-do
how natural a birth

I know it is ok
all the time I knew
now they will see it
It all went True

Featured Contributors

Dawn Zehren

Dawn Zehren is a speaker, coach, strategist, and overall instigator. For more than 20 years, Dawn has helped individual and company clients get clear about what they genuinely want, and then has provided the structure of support for them to create it. Their results range from homes to happiness, from self-confidence to sales and success. Dawn's motto is "Together we go further faster."

Her passions include percolating ideas, laughing out loud, creating concepts and crafts, bursting into song, sharing stories and meals, and celebrating others. Dawn lives in beautiful Wauwatosa (MKE), Wisconsin, with her husband, Nick, and their "four-legged boy" (dog), Jack.

Deborah Servetnick

Deborah Servetnick has been a transformational teacher all her adult life, following a path that could only be designed by divine guidance, connecting everything. Deborah grew up in Philadelphia, and her love of the Grateful Dead brought her to Berkeley in 1980, where she began her study of bodywork, Chinese medicine, breathwork, meditation, and the human energy field. Her deeply intuitive healing practice led her to work with people with AIDS and other life threatening illness, and while engaged as an Act-Up activist in San Francisco and Philadelphia, she continued in spiritual study to hold space for the dying and their transition.

By the time she was 30 Deborah studied with Wayne Dyer, Louise Hay, and Marianne Williamson; returning to psychedelic substances for expanded consciousness, and experienced her first ayahuasca ceremony, and met the Dalai Lama. But it was during a Dark Night of the Soul breast cancer experience in 2011 when she was teaching high school English that her communication with the spirit world accelerated.

Deborah was led to join a groundbreaking psychedelic research study for cancer patients with end-of-life anxiety at JHU. It reset her life. You can hear Deborah's story in a movie from Unlimited Sciences https://unlimitedsciences.org/breast-cancer-psychedelics-and-end-of-life-anxiety-a-survivors-story/ and today, Grateful Deb is a Certified Life Mastery Coach, a renowned public speaker, and has taught and empowered thousands to move from a conditional life to a life they love living through a transformational spiritual curriculum in alignment with a psychedelic experience, using the same tools that saved her life. Deb has worked to see Initiative 81 in DC a success. Psychedelic medicine offers relief to Veterans and others with PTSD, offers cancer patients healing, and has alleviated depression and chronic headaches.

Contact Deborah for information on individual and group classes and retreats at deb@gratefuldeb.com. Please check the laws in your state; Deborah reminds you this is a changing landscape and she does not advocate or provide illegal substances. https://psychedelicoach.com

Didi Selwa

Didi Selwa grew up at Redondo Beach in Southern California. She spent her days basking in the sunshine with her head buried in a book. Her book interests range from fun beach reads to meaningful personal development. As her passion for personal and spiritual growth expanded, it opened up a whole new way of living.

After the company she had worked for over 25 years unexpectedly closed her department, she decided to pursue her passion for helping others. She found her purpose as a certified transformational life coach and launched her business. Her life-changing workshops and programs help people break through their limiting beliefs, achieve greater results, and learn to live with passion and purpose.

When she is not growing her highly successful coaching business, you can find her either practicing yoga or enjoying time with her precious dog Ty.

Erin Davenport

Erin Davenport brings a dynamic background of being a published inspirational author in numerous magazines, the CEO of Light of the Traveler, a Certified Life Mastery Coach, an international speaker, and she enjoys leading retreats as well as trips overseas to support her volunteer organization in Kenya that she started during college, over ten years ago.

Being a past overachiever painfully underachieving, she enjoys authentically sharing hope through her personal journey of overcoming. She believes in the power within us all to achieve what our ingrained belief systems may label as impossible.

Her passion and purpose is walking with people during their sacred journey of defining and creating a life they love living. Erin's coaching sweet spot is helping people step into a career or entrepreneurial venture that gives them fulfillment or to flourish within their current vocation. She also cherishes her two Bengal cat brothers, Reptar and Hyrax. You can discover more about Erin at www.lightofthetraveler.com.

Gina Eubank

Gina Eubank specializes in helping entrepreneurs grow their business while creating a life they love.

A licensed Pharmacist, results and mindset expert, a certified Life Mastery Consultant, speaker, coach and mentor Gina is distinctly qualified in what she calls, "Doing the Do." She has spent years learning and living this concept and teaching people how to get maximum leverage in their business and their life through vision, commitment, emotional perseverance, consistency and knowing how and when to pivot for maximum impact and results.

Faced with surgery for a brain tumor in 2003, Gina made the courageous decision to take herself off 11 RX drugs in order to cleanse, detox and to learn and apply new mindset tools to help her heal. In 8 short months she was 100% healed and off all 11 RX's.

Knowing if she could do this with her health, she could do this in every area of her life! Gina decoded and created a system and roadmap that is effective and repeatable and yields massive results for anyone who implements the system.

She is dedicated to helping anyone become the person they MOST want to become and empowering them with this system of transformation and tools to achieve their dream results.

Janet Langmeier

For 30 plus years, Janet Langmeier has worked with organizations and individuals, helping them build their dreams, accelerate their results, and create richer, more fulfilling lives.

A sought-after speaker, teacher, and coach, Janet Langmeier has offered transformational workshops to organizations around the country.

As a Certified Life Mastery Consultant and Transformational Life Coach, Janet's work blends spiritual principles with practical real-world applications. She helps you connect with the infinite side of your nature where you create extraordinary results in all areas of your life.

Katherine Loranger

Transformational Life Coach and founder of Katalyst Coaching, Katherine Loranger asserts to the bold and determined that life is theirs for the taking.

For over 25 years, Katherine has been driven to spark lasting, heartfelt transformation for fearless and fierce souls in process—working to research, study, and implement results-oriented principles and programs to incredible success.

Through her evocative and expertly-guided series of vision building and life mastery classes and workshops, heart-centered entrepreneurs, organizational leaders, and dreamers learn to realign their efforts and energies with their soul's purpose to design, build, and realize their wildest fantasies—igniting a world of limitless possibilities and changing the trajectory of their lives, their businesses, and their relationships for the better.

Laura Corkery

For over 13 years, Laura Corkery has studied transformational principles and helped people build their dreams, accelerate their results, and create more vibrant and fulfilling lives. Laura is an experienced facilitator, sought-after speaker, and the founder and CEO of True You Living.

Laura has more than 18 years of experience, leading teams and creating inclusive cultures in Fortune 50 companies. She has presented at national Diversity & Inclusion conferences and received numerous awards for her D&I leadership. She has over ten years of ERG leadership experience and has created national and global ally programs.

Laura's superpower is challenging the status quo, and she is passionate about creating a world that embraces all. Laura earned her B.S. in Industrial Distribution from Texas A&M University and is a certified Life Mastery Consultant. She lives in Dallas with her husband, Scott, and two young children.

Marilyn K. Lawrence

Marilyn K. Lawrence is a DreamBuilder Coach, certified with The Brave Thinking Institute. Marilyn's transformational workshops and one-on-one trainings facilitate the dynamic process of manifesting treasured dreams.

Marilyn is an ambassador for a world business leader and has garnered rich experience at other prominent organizations including the U.S. Department of Labor. She co-authored *On the Wings of Faith,* and her daybook, *Office Confidential,* is scheduled for release in 2022.

Martha Grier

Martha Grier is a native New Yorker of African-American and German heritage. She is the founder of Still, I Rise Coaching, which provides resilience-based, personal leadership and wellness coaching services. Bringing over 20 years of experience as a consultant for Fortune 500 financial firms, Martha helps professionals in the second half of life heal their past, reclaim their power, pursue their passion, and fulfill their desire to live a life of meaning, joy, freedom, and wellness.

Martha lives along the Hudson River and enjoys cooking, reading, writing, listening to jazz, and taking meditative walks in the woods near her home.

Patricia Campbell

Patricia Campbell is a Transformational Life and Business coach whose passion is empowering women to create lives they absolutely LOVE LIVING! She offers coaching that integrates spiritual principles with practical, everyday applications to help her clients break through their paradigms and manifest the results they desire to live richer, more fulfilling lives.

Patricia has studied success principles, personal development, and spirituality for more than 30 years with world-renowned teachers such as Mary Morrissey, Lisa Nichols, Gary Zukav, and Gabor Mate. Utilizing this expertise, she offers inspiring interactive workshops, transformational in-depth coaching programs, and keynote speeches to help women achieve new heights of success, fulfillment, aliveness, and freedom!

Raquel Hernandez-Meyer

Raquel Hernandez-Meyer is a certified Transformational Trainer and Life Mastery Consultant. She is passionate about helping people feel alive again by getting crystal clear about what the life of their dreams looks like, learn how to ask for what they truly love, and take consistent action steps until they manifest their dreams.

Raquel shares her own personal experience to demonstrate that it is possible to navigate out of the darkest period of your life when you stay connected to your vision.

Raquel wholeheartedly believes and demonstrates that living your dreams depends on the embodiment and practice of transformational tools, not on the conversations or lectures about them. "Exemplar" is what Neale Donald Walsh called Raquel during a direct interaction with her at his May 2018 retreat in Oregon, while Raquel was on stage being vulnerable and sharing about her divorce.

Samantha Kaaua

Samantha Kaaua is an Author, Professional Keynote Speaker, Marriage Coach for Women, and Licensed Marriage & Family Therapist. She is the author of *Creating Your Marriage Miracle*, a new age guide to Transforming Your Relationship, Saving Your Family and Fulfilling Your Destiny. Since 2014, Samantha has worked with, guided, and successfully mentored upwards of 1000 individuals and couples to transform their marriage and achieve their dreams.

She is a world-leading authority on creating healthy relationships and specializes in empowering women to have clarity, confidence, and connection in their marriages. Samantha always says, "it only takes one person to transform your marriage" and has discovered innovative ways to do just that by saving her own marriage years ago.

Samantha was born and raised and currently resides with her incredibly supportive husband and three amazing daughters in Honolulu, Hawaii.

Susan Kennedy

As a Life Mastery Consultant and Transformation Coach after 20 years in corporate America, Susan Kennedy understands how easy it is for women to sacrifice their own needs, dreams, and desires for everyone else. In doing so, they are in effect sacrificing themselves, their health, their well-being, their creative talents, their resources, energy, and money all because they feel like they are doing what they "should." When they realize the depths of their unhappiness despite external appearances, they start to realize they don't really know who they are anymore or what they really want.

Committed to the process and depth of rediscovery, drawing out the innate and buried treasures in each woman and clearing the paradigms that led to this point, Susan has studied with dozens of thought leaders, coaches, and spiritual mentors to give the guidance and support she offers her clients. Once awakened to that power and creativity within, that's when we truly are home.

Susan knows how to shift stubborn one-sided perceptions that keep us stuck and spinning. Using a proven method to tap into what matters most to you, she supports you to create a redesigned and re-envisioned life for yourself. In addition to the beach and pickleball, her passion is teaching clients to unlock their true potential, achieve outrageous happiness, and live a life they LOVE living!

Made in the USA
Columbia, SC
04 August 2021